Watermark:
Leaving a Life-long Stain

Mission Trip Discipleship Plan
30 Devotionals Written by
Mission Trip Veterans

Bobby Loukinen

Project manager / Editor-in-chief: Bobby Loukinen

General Editor: Lyn Gwost

Cover Art: istockphoto

Cover Design: Jake Hemmesch

Published in Little Falls, MN by ES Sports

Acknowledgements

sus Christ - for Salvation and giving me a purpose in life.

n – my wife of 21 years who is helping me raise four world-changing children. Thanks for
eing so supportive of my dreams over the years, for believing in me, and for really being
y best friend...I'm blessed!

ke, Riley, Rachel and Alex – for being the most amazing kids I could ever ask for. I am
ways so very proud of you, and I feel incredibly blessed to be called Dad.

ob and Naomi Loukinen (my parents) – for raising me in a healthy home, and for setting a
odly example for me to follow.

on Tennant – the most influential youth Pastor (of the seven) during my teen years.
hanks for believing in me, for not letting me do too many stupid things, and for speaking
to my life so often in your very honest and unique style. Sorry for decorations I left in
our yard over the years - the bags of leaves, left over Christmas trees, forks, spoons,
nives, the countless bags of flour that left notes on your grass, and for the rolls of toilet
aper that numbered in the hundreds that I forgot in your trees.

od Kimbler – the first pastor to give me an opportunity to work with his youth group. He
 now enjoying his treasures in heaven. You are greatly missed! May he rest in peace.

eith Thompson – for being a great friend over the year, and for giving me a second chance
s a youth pastor after my first real youth pastorate ended disastrously..

wenty-nine Authors – It has been a privilege to watch you grow in your faith since I first
net you. It has been inspiring to watch you grow in faith from your teen years to an adult,
hriving in your walk with the Lord, rather than just going through the motions. The
stains" of the mission trip are still evident in your life!

yn Gwost – for doing a fantastic job editing this project. It was quite the job with 30
ifferent writers all bringing a different writing style.

hanks to the hundreds and hundreds of Powerhouse and Motion students over the years
or listening to me week after week and for taking my challenges to heart and stepping out
n faith to change your world. I was always so proud to call you "my guys!"

Forward

have known Bobby Loukinen for the past 16 years. In all that time, several things stick ut to me: Bobby is coach, a friend, a disciple, and maker of disciples. He is an athlete ithout the ego. He is an example of servant leadership.

hen I first met Bobby, he was working out of a smaller church with limited funds. He did ot let limited resources keep him from challenging students to live out their faith beyond e church building. He trained and invested time in students. For 18 years, class after ass of students would come out of his youth ministry ready for a larger world, grounded their faith in Christ. Many went on to become pastors, missionaries, doctors, teachers nd more.

think it was easier for students to follow in Bobby's footsteps because he led by example. e did not ask them to do something he had not done or wasn't willing to do. He was ways walking ahead of them.

obby has a big heart for missions. Whether it is some place on the other side of the world across the street, Bobby is teaching his students to prepare and reach out. They did and till are!

obby Loukinen's ministry has produced students who have been directly involved with innesota Youth Alive and reaching students. Now, I see them involved with ministry as dults - a sign of great discipleship. This book is an outgrowth of years of practical ministry students that caused them move beyond knowing the Bible to living out what it says.

ichard Baker
xecutive Director
innesota Youth Alive

Contents

How to Use this book

s you look forward to an exciting mission trip embarking on, my desire is that this trip aves a "**watermark**", a permanent stain, on your life! How deep or permanent that stain oes, I believe, depends on how committed you are to allowing God to permeate your life nd your habits. In this Watermark discipleship program, you will be challenged to stablish a daily habit of spending time with God - both in prayer and reading as well as nemorizing His word. These habits can leave permanent stains on your life and can help trengthen and establish a life-long habit of pursuing God.

he requirements of Watermark:
 Read one devotional per day (6 per week), answer the questions in the Daily Watermark hallenge with more than a one-word answer, put some thought into your responses.

 Read 1 - 2 chapters of the Old Testament, 1 - 2 chapters of the New Testament, and 1 – 2 salms and a Proverb each day.

 Memorize the two key scriptures per week; i.e., 10 over the five weeks. (page 101)

 Daily time in prayer, Goal - Ten minutes or more, praying the revolving calendar page 99) praying for your team, trip leaders, ministry host / ministry, that God would repare you, etc.

 Develop your story of what God has done in your life to share with family and friends. It an also be publicly shared on the trip.

 Find a coach to help you stay accountable to this commitment of establishing the habits f praying, living and telling in your life. (Page 98, a form your coach can look at and sign)

n the back of the book, there are charts to help you track the progress of your daily Bible eading, scripture memorization, and the revolving prayer calendar.

These trips are often the greatest time of spiritual growth in a person's life because for nany people, it is the first time they have ever stepped out in faith to share what God has lone for them. Additionally, the experience fosters the opportunity for individuals to step utside their comfort zone and truly rely on God. The "stain" can be more than a two-week vent; it can become a lifetime of living at a level of pursuing a relationship with Jesus Christ

So, you have a choice to make. Will it be a great experience where you will have some inforgettable moments and killer photos to go along with your souvenirs, OR will it be the tart of living a life dependent upon God, regularly stepping out in faith and routinely going utside of your comfort zone?

Introduction

have vivid memories of my first mission trip; I traveled to England and Scotland. I clearly remember standing in the immigration line at Gatwick airport outside of London, not sure what the next two weeks would hold. I was both extremely excited and rather fearful of the unknown; I had no idea of what to expect with this being my first visit outside the friendly confines of the United States.

Standing in line with my carry-on bag and my passport in hand, I suddenly thought, AM I READY FOR THIS? I knew what the schedule said would happen, but I was wondering if what so many other people said about mission trips would happen to me. Before the trip, many people would ask what we had planned on the trip, and most people would go on to share some story about a mission trip they went on that didn't turn out exactly as it was planned. Looking back, the trip didn't exactly happen as it was planned. There were countless changes, but that is what I loved about that first trip; I wasn't in charge of anything. I had to be flexible and adapt to many changes, and maybe for the first time in my life, I truly relied on God.

Getting a firsthand look at a new culture, laughing at some crazy British accents, riding the tube all over London, exploring Westminster Abbey and other historic sites around the city, was an amazing experience for me. One of the coolest places I visited was the Edinburgh castle in Scotland at the end of the famed Royal Mile; I absolutely loved it! Exploring all these new places opened up a Pandora Box of passion in my life for new cultures and new experiences. On top of all the cultural aspects, having an opportunity to talk about my faith in schools and in churches was probably my favorite part of the trip. I felt like God was opening my eyes to exciting plans He had in store for my future. I didn't realize then what a big part of my life missions would become, for now I'm a fulltime home missionary, I direct a mission organization, and I have participated in 24 mission trips. I LOVE missions!

During my years as a youth pastor, I had the privilege of taking hundreds of students on trips around the world to share the life-giving message of Jesus Christ. Together we've seen the tropics, rainforests, frozen places as well as the midnight sun, Caribbean islands, architectural marvels, pyramids, big cities, small rural towns, and places that were recovering from a Hurricane, and I've loved it all! Every trip has left indelible images in my mind. I can recall stories of exciting ministry opportunities with students experiencing things for the first times and many victories, as well as defeats. This book contains a few of these stories.

There are 29 additional authors to this book, each one a participant on an AIM trip (Ambassadors in Missions). They each had a similar experience as I did in the immigration line at the Gatwick airport, a realization that they had no idea of what to expect. They all faced similar fears and feelings of inadequacy, all were unsure if God could use them and their limited skills. I can speak with first hand knowledge to this fact, because each author is a former student that traveled with me somewhere in the world. I am so proud of them taking this step of faith by authoring a devotional to help the next generation of mission trip participants prepare themselves for the adventure that lies ahead.

Only one author has been published before, so there is practically zero writing experience in the crowd, which is amazing once you read these devotionals. They all speak candidly from personal experience about their successes and failures and the lessons they learned from their trip. As you read these daily devotionals, realize a student just like you writes it only a few years older. They sat in the same classes you presently sit in, went to the same youth ministry conventions and camps you did, and, have experienced what you are about to experience. They stepped out. God blessed them with an incredible faith-growing experience, and they have never been the same since. The habits of praying, living, and telling that they established before the trip, still help them to continue to grow in their relationship with the Lord today.

So, it's time to face your fears and step out into faith on the trip, for I'm confident God has some cool things in store for you!

Bobby Loukinen
January 2014

Chapter 1

Watermark

Stains

Everyone has stains in their life, moments that have been both good and bad, events that will forever be with us, for these events shape our lives.

I was eight years old when a poor choice left a permanent stain on my life. I'm not sure what kind of home you were raised in, but I had the privilege of growing up in a Godly home that produced a healthy family. My mom and dad placed a high priority on living a life according to the standards laid out in the Bible, and we attended church as often as the doors were open; church attendance was never an option for me. I was 20 years old before I watched the entire Super Bowl because it happens on Sunday, and church is always scheduled for that night. I'm not complaining; that's just the way it was.

Even though I was born into a great family and knew the "Right" way to live, but I was far from perfect. Looking back at my childhood, I had some anger issues. I remember going upstairs many times to my room after my mom and I had a one-sided argument. I always lost these arguments, and I would find myself so mad at her. I would storm up the stairs and then pace back and forth letting anger boil up inside of me. I would have thoughts racing through my mind. Comments I wanted to say to my mom filed my mind, but I could never get those words out. I could call it fear or I could call it respect, for respect was always stressed in my family. The importance of respecting parents, pastors, police

officers, and everyone in authority was expected in my household. There was a constan
point of emphasis in our house; it was to treat others as you want to be treated.

Anger management was not one of my finest characteristics as a kid, and a few of these
one-sided arguments with my mom ended in disaster for me. There is still a patched hole
in the wall of my parents' home outside of the door that led up to my room from one failed
attempt of dealing with my anger. Now, don't get the wrong impression of me; I'm not a
ticking time bomb or some ranting and raving, out of control sports fanatic. However, as an
eight year old, I didn't really know how to control my anger yet, but God had a lesson for
me just around the next corner.

Most of the rough times of my childhood are cloudy but I do have vivid memories of how
God used one conflict to really get my attention and leave a permanent stain on my life. My
mom was performing her motherly duties, loving me enough to correct things I was doing
wrong - probably concerning my negative attitude - and we had another argument. I don't
exactly remember how it all took place, but I'm sure it involved my mom lecturing me
again; I'm sure I was so mad as usual, that I was about to explode. Once again, I'm sure I
wasn't even able to form words to talk back to her, and I did the same thing I always
did...storm off, up the stairs, to my room. In order to get to my room, I had to open a door
to the stairs, which led to my escape from the situation. I opened the door, stepped inside
and since I wanted to make a dramatic exit with a loud statement to my mom of how mad I
was at her, I decided to slam the door. I did a fantastic job of slamming the door shut that
day without much of a sound; I had slammed the door on my thumb.

I remember clearly how my anger quickly shifted to extreme pain. I had done a great job of
slamming the door directly on my fingernail resulting in a throbbing pain. I didn't make it
up to my room that day to sulk away in anger; instead I stayed right there along side the
person that had just seconds before had been making me so mad. She was now consoling
me and getting some ice.

My thumb swelled up to almost cartoon-size that day; it was so huge! My mom knew there
was not much she could do except ice it, so we piled into the car and drove to the
emergency room. I could describe to you in great detail, things I saw and felt in the ER that
day. Medical equipment, instruments, smells & sounds, created an experience that would
change my life.

A nurse brought us back to an examination room and performed all the duties nurses do;
such as asking many questions about how it happened, and taking my blood pressure, and
my temperature. I was taken to an x-ray room, and photos were shot of my damaged
thumb. After a few minutes of waiting, I saw the doctor walk up to the door, which was
shielded by the curtain, he was looking at an x-ray and reading the chart, and then I heard
hushed whispers between the doctor and nurse. The doctor entered the room confidently
and introduced himself. He reviewed the situation out loud with us, reading off notes
written by the nurse, asking questions of my mom and myself. The doctor then said, "We
are going to take care of that thumb," leaving the room to pick up whatever a doctor needs
to take care of a battered thumb.

When the doctor walked back into the room with the supplies he was obviously planning on using, I was shocked and slightly confused. He didn't bring in some sophisticated instruments with shiny parts, but only a candle, a lighter, and a paperclip. He then took the lighter, lit the candle and started to bend the paperclip. I was watching, confused about what was happening. It was nothing like I saw on TV. He took the paperclip with one side bent straight and put it in the fire of the candle. After a few seconds, he turned to me and explained what needed to happen. He said, "You have a lot of fluid trapped under your thumbnail which is causing you a lot of pain. I'm going to use this paperclip I sterilized in the fire to release that pressure. It may hurt a little bit, but then, I promise you, it will feel much better." Then the doctor asked me a rhetorical question: "Are you ready?"

What happened next was both amazing and horrible all in the same moment. He took the red-hot paperclip and pierced my thumbnail. I was expecting it to be insanely painful, but it didn't hurt a bit. After it went through my nail very easily, he pulled it back out. It was awesome to watch. He pulled out the paperclip from my thumbnail and a stream of fluid shot clear over my head; it looked like a water fountain. He repeated the process to burn a second hole in my nail and then the horrible part happened. The doctor took my thumb and around my first knuckle down from the nail, started to apply pressure to push all the extra-pooled fluid out of the newly formed exit wounds. This is the part that hurt really badly, but being a tough 8-year-old kid, I was determined not to cry. I wasn't so tough after all; I melted under the pressure and cried like a baby. Coming to rescue me from my pain, my mom, the target of my anger, lovingly held me as I buried my head on her shoulder until the pain was under control.

I had an anger issue, but God had a plan. He allowed my anger to bring me to a place where I was ready to learn from my mistake. Did God make me slam the door on my finger? No, He simply allowed my immaturity to bring about a needed change in my life. After that horrible day in the summer between my second and third grade year, I learned how to handle my anger much better. Do I still get angry? Absolutely, but I haven't slammed a door in anger in many, many years. God allowed a horrible situation to be used as a great teaching moment in my life. I will forever have a stain on my life because of my reaction and that stupid upstairs door.

Commitment

In my lifetime, I've had an incredible opportunity to spend thousands and thousands of hours with teens, and for over 18 years, I had the title of youth pastor. I really loved being a youth pastor! One observation I noticed over time is that the teen years are filled with moments that ABC's, Wide World of Sports describe as, "the thrill of victory and the agony of defeat". There can be many ups and downs in your life, even during the same day. The teen years are filled with times of discovery and exploration and trial and error. It's also a time to test parental limits and try to figure out where your own limits will be set. Overall, they can be some great years of your life! I've watched many students make some incredibly stupid choices and watched a lot make really great choices too. One choice I've been particularly excited to be apart of is watching students go one their first mission trip.

Over the years, I've had the privilege of going on 24 mission trips with hundreds of students, and I've realized, it's one of the highlights of my life. Watching a student experience a different culture while experiencing an attitude change about so many things in their life is invigorating to me. I absolutely love going on trips with students!

My window of influence as a youth pastor in my most recent church (shout out to my peeps at LHC!) was between the 7th and 12th grade in a student's life. I did everything I could to try and instill a heart for missions during their journey through our ministry. I routinely stressed the importance of giving to missions, for Matthew 6:21(NIV) says, "For where your treasure is, there your heart will be also." I knew that if I could get students to give money to a mission project, it would speak volumes to where their heart truly was. I do realize money is a pretty important part of a student's life, for they can do a lot with their money. They can go out to eat with friends, download the latest songs or games, or purchase the latest clothes, shoes, or sneakers to keep up their image. I knew they had a lot of choices to make with how they were going to spend their money, and if they gave it willingly in an offering for a mission project, their heart was most likely in the right place.

In my opinion, what's more important than a student's money is their time and commitment. I figured out over many years of ministry that if I could get a student to sacrifice some of their time and their money for a specific project, I really knew their heart was right. It was the unique combination of those two precious commodities of a student that created a telling formula. Time + money = Life change! That is what I would call the start of a mission trip experience - a true spiritual equation of God's anointing (commitment + time + money + God = a life changing experience).

If you are reading this book, it most likely means you are planning to go on a mission trip sometime in the next few months. Get ready, the experience can change your life!

Watermark

While on the island of St. Maarten during a cruise with my wife, I walked passed an old wooden ship in dry dock. As I stopped to take a closer look, it very easy to see how low it had sat in the water for a long, long time. The ocean saltwater had started to eat away the paint on the wooden hull, and it was starting to rot. The water had left a permanent stain on the side of the ship; it left a stain at the highest point of the connection between the water and the ship's hull. I'm no expert on the ocean or boating; I'm not even a fisherman, but to me, that is what I would call a watermark.

The mission trip experience for most teens (not all of them though) can be the "high watermark" of their spiritual walk with Christ. It's common for a student to share their faith for the very first time publicly while on a trip, oftentimes they are bold, even daring in what they try and accomplish for the Kingdom.

The danger of a mission trip is that it lasts only a few weeks. Then it's over. The boldness that students walked in is done when they return to the same routine of going through the motions in their walk with Christ upon returning from the trip. They return to the same abits that didn't inspire them to greatness or dependence of God but rather to sort of easting. My prayer is that your mission trip is more than a few weeks high, but rather a art of a continuously growing relationship with Christ.

ve grown immensely in stature, maturity, and faith since I was a young boy of just eight ears. The pain of a crushed thumb was temporary, but the watermark on my life has ecome a permanent reminder in my walk of faith with Christ. I've chosen an honest estyle of developing positive life habits – an acquired behavior pattern regularly llowed. My prayer is that your mission trip is more than a high point for a few weeks. I ray it is the start of a growing relationship with Christ.

Chapter 2

Live It Out Loud

Who you are is more important than what you can do! If your upcoming mission trip is going to have a significant "watermark" on your life, you need to have some training habits in place before the trip begins, routines that help your continual spiritual growth. I have seen many students who did very little to prepare themselves for their trip, and on the first day of the experience, they were overwhelmed with the seriousness of this trip and the spiritual climate it entailed. I've watched as kids realized, they had nothing in their "spiritual tank" to give to others because their own relationship was not where it needed to be. Consequently, the first few days of the trip end up being spent getting things right in their own personal relationship with the Lord, versus being ready to minister and serve others.

"I need to be in training before the trips begins?" you may be asking yourself. The answer is: YES! Have you ever played a sport or played an instrument in the band, or maybe had a part in the school play? If so, you always have rehearsals or practices before the night of the game or performance. People don't just "show up" for their big night on the court or in the arts. Instead, everyone has to go into training to prepare them for the event; mission trips are no different.

I was twelve years old when I tackled my first racing event, a 5k around Lake Harriet in Minneapolis, Minnesota. It was a fund-raiser for a local crisis pregnancy center and adoption agency. I remember that Saturday in May for it was a beautiful day. It was pretty warm with a light breeze blowing off the lake - a really great day for a run. Leading up t the race, I thought I was in pretty good shape because I was a pretty active kid. My dail routine after school would be to go on a bike ride and take some sick jumps on my BM bike, come home and eat, and then either play basketball or wiffle ball with other kids i the neighborhood. I was in the midst of my last season of Little League baseball too. Whe I got to the band shell that morning to check in as a participant for the race, I felt prett confident in what I was about to do; I was expecting to perform pretty well, maybe eve win this race.

As the runners approached the starting line, I looked around and found myself amon about 150 other runners. Many had the latest styles in running gear with the newes models of running shoes. I had an old pair of canvas Nikes, not exactly as old as the P flyers made famous by the movie *Sandlot*, but they were not far removed either. I didn have the latest in running gear either. I had an old Minnesota Twins t-shirt, and for som reason, a pair of white sweat pants with a pretty tight pair of blue shorts over them. wasn't sure, but the thought hit me for the first time, I might be in trouble this mornin Could I really compete with these other runners?

I had gone on exactly zero runs before I lined up for my first race. I had run a lot in baseba practice and basketball games, and even had ridden my bike for many, many miles, but had failed to run just to run. I lined up, the gun went off, and I quickly ran to the front of th pack along with one of my friends (also fashionably dressed that morning. The shorts ove the sweats was his idea). We were both leading the race, and in my mind I thought, this i pretty easy. Before I even got to the end of the parking lot a few hundred feet from th starting line, something happened. The first adult caught me, effortlessly running past m in perfect form. He was soon joined by a few more, and then almost everyone else caugh me and passed me over the next few hundred yards. I thought I was doing ok, but I coul start to feel a pain in my stomach, just above my right hip.   That small pain grew into sharp pain, then into an almost debilitating pain that stopped me from running and mad me walk. I looked back, and I was about a half of mile from the band shell, about two and half miles left to the finish line. My ego took quite a hit that day when a few ladies in th sixties or seventies ran (or should I say shuffled past me) as I struggled to walk and eve breath.

I couldn't understand what was going on. I thought I was in great shape; I was very activ and played baseball and biked almost every day. I had an unrealistic opinion of where was physically. I thought I could just show up and do pretty well, maybe even win the rac but I was not at all ready to compete in the 5k that day because I had not done any trainin ahead of time. My body was not in the practice of running those distances.

As you look forward to the mission trip, you can't just show up like I did at the start of th race, thinking everything was ok, because it doesn't work that way. You need to go int training as you approach the trip and establish routines or habits that will prepare you t be used by God to minister and bless those He is sending you to serve. Routines or habit that will take care of issues you have in your relationship with the Lord ahead of tim should be established, so you don't show up on the trip and struggle through it personall ming back spiritually defeated. "Who you are is more important than what you can do" is ry true when it comes to mission trips. Being spiritually ready for the trip is more iportant than what can be done publicly.

Live It / Live It Out Loud

ere is my definition of this phrase:

ve It – describes the qualities of a person internally: passion, honesty, integrity, and irity of the heart.

ive it out loud – describes what a person does publically: sharing the faith, loving and rving others.

you live out loud what you don't have inside, in my opinion, that's hypocrisy and being ke. Over the years, I've seen many people arrive on trips with little spiritual training ead of time, and they are simply not very effective on the trip because they cannot give way spiritually what they don't already posses themselves. To establish routines of irsuing your relationship with the Lord is of UTMOST importance before the trip begins. on't wait until the trip starts to begin this process because that leads to a lot of regrets hen you look back on your trip.

Live It – The Word

his routine or habit works on your relationship with the Lord internally. It's a powerful ractice to read the Bible daily with this question in mind:

someone were to ask you today, "What did God speak to you about in your time in is word?" How would you answer them?

on't just read the Bible; read it so you can apply it to issues you are dealing with in life. od's word is a game plan for your life. I've heard it said, "Every issue in life that you could truggle with is addressed in the Bible." Answers exist for everything you could be going irough in life, but you can't find those answers unless you do more than just read it. Read ie Bible as instructions on how to live because it is! James 1:22 says, "Do not merely listen) the word and so deceive yourself, do what it says." God inspired 40 authors over a 1600 ear period of time to write the books of the Bible - not just to record history - but to rovide words from God that bring life, encouragement, and freedom from those who are ddicted and live in bondage. The words of the Bible can literally save peoples life by iving them hope. It can be so much more than a history book. It is the book written for ou through divine inspiration. II Timothy 3:16 says, "All Scripture is God-breathed and is seful for teaching, rebuking, correcting and training in righteousness." If you want to row spiritually, you MUST dive into God's word daily. On page 100 in the back of this ook, you will find a 12-week reading plan for the New Testament. Remember, don't just ead it to cross it off your list of things to do today, but rather read it to get a word from the ord that can help get you through areas of your life you may be struggling with personally. lis word was written for you!

Live It – Prayer

This routine or habit builds your relationship with the Lord internally as well. Prayer can be both a ritual and a habit; it's the energy behind the prayer that makes the difference in my opinion. There are great rituals in prayer that are meaningful and impactful: praying over your food before a meal, thanking God for providing the meal, and praying for the hands that have prepared it = great stuff! Praying a memorized prayer with your children before they go to bed at night = amazing! Reciting the Lord's Prayer at the end of a service = a great reminder of what God has done for our lives and what He may have in store for you in the days ahead. The danger for me, in those instances, is that it is just a routine; think very little about the meaning of what I am saying. Those can be powerful words without much thought, effort, or sincerity behind them; I think the effectiveness could be a little lacking. Now don't get mad at me, I am NOT saying memorized prayers are bad or even ineffective, I'm rather saying you might stunt your spiritual growth a bit if that's all you do. My favorite definition of prayer is that it is a conversation between two people who love each other.

When I pray, I don't picture God as some distant entity that I need to impress with my intelligent words or even my list of good deeds I have performed, but rather, a God who is personally interested in every area of my life. God is one I can honestly share my thoughts, feelings, frustration and struggles with. I don't want to over-humanize God, like I can invite Him over to my house at 7pm to split a strawberry smoothie and eat some chips and cheese while playing chess together, but I do want to remind you that "He is a friend that sticks closer than any brother" as stated in Proverbs 18:24. The Bible describes God as one who has been tempted in every way we have. Hebrews 4:15-16 says, "For we do not have a high priest who is unable to empathize with our weaknesses, but we have one who has been tempted in every way, just as we are—yet he did not sin. Let us then approach God's throne of grace with confidence, so that we may receive mercy and find grace to help us in our time of need." When I pray, I want to visualize the Lord, leaning forward on His throne, listening to every word I say, ready to act as a result of my asking Him to. A few sayings that have stuck with me over the years regarding prayer are: **Every prayer that is not asked goes unanswered**. **Prayer always has an affect, No prayer always has an affect.**

To make prayer apart of your daily routine is key to your spiritual growth. In the back of this book (page 99) you will find a revolving prayer calendar. Fill out this with someone or something to pray about each day in your personal life, your school, and your upcoming trip. It will help keep you focused on what you feel like you should be praying for on any given day of the month. I challenge you to start making time in conversation with God a priority each day; it will change your life!

Live It - Out Loud

The quote at the beginning of this chapter, "Who you are is more important than what you do" is very true, but if all you did in your relationship with the Lord is Read His word, and Pray, there would be a many missed opportunities to influence those around you. James 2:14-17 speaks to this issue, "What good is it, my brothers and sisters, if someone claims to ve faith but has no deeds? Can such faith save them? Suppose a brother or a sister is without clothes and daily food. If one of you says to them, "Go in peace; keep warm and well fed" but does nothing about their physical needs, what good is it? In the same way, **faith by itself, if it is not accompanied by action, is dead.**   Faith without any actions is dead. The Message version of James 2: 17 says, "Isn't it obvious that God-talk without God-acts is outrageous nonsense?" You must combine the time in the word and prayer with actual deeds, or tangible things that can help meet the needs of those around you. That would be "Living It Out Loud!"

Live It Out Loud – The Power of Your Story

I've been asked questions countless times in my lifetime. How would you answer it? How do you know God is real?") There are many responses you might have. You could highlight the four spiritual laws or move into an Evangelism Explosion presentation or come up with some other method of explaining the Gospel. The best way to answer that question is to talk about what God has done for you personally. I have a lot of stories of God's protection I could share or stories about students I knew that overcame horrific circumstances to thrive in life because of a relationship with Jesus Christ.

My favorite story to share is about my aunt. She has been a pastor's wife for many years. She was 30 years old, and the doctors discovered that she had cancer. At home were three small children, my cousins. They did many tests and tried many different treatments to stave off the aggressive cancer in her body, she also had surgery to remove her Thyroid as well. The doctors concluded that there were no other options for her to pursue. With nowhere else to turn, my Uncle and Aunt turned to a God they had been preaching about in their church and cried out for God to intervene and do something miraculous. I was not yet born, so this is all second-hand information, but I know the story well. It was an ordinary Sunday at their church, and after the worship time and preaching of the word, they gathered in front to end the service in prayer. My Aunt had been prayed for many times before, but once again she requested the church pray for her in her desperate situation. Matthew 18:19-20 says, "Again, truly I tell you that if two of you on earth agree about anything they ask for, it will be done for them by my Father in Heaven. For where two or three gather in my name, there am I with them." They gathered around her once again and agreed in prayer like they had done many times before. Nothing spectacular happened that night, and they shut off the lights and everyone went home.

Little did the people who gathered to pray that night know what God had done in my Aunt's body until the following week. It was once again time for a follow up with her doctor to track the progression of this aggressive cancer. She went in for X-Rays as she had done many times before. To her amazement, she was called back to the hospital to meet with her doctor. He held in his hands two sets of X-Rays, one dated weeks earlier and one with the most current date on it. The doctor then compared the two photographs describing what he saw in the first one, and what he could not find any sign of in the second photo. The cancer was evident on the first X-Ray, for she was "lit up like a Christmas tree" as I've heard it described many times in my family over the years. On the second X-Ray, there was no sign of any cancer, which was unexplainable for the doctor.

I know what happened, and it didn't happen in the doctor's office that day with a malfunctioning machine or some misreading of some medical data. It happened the previous Sunday, at the end of a service up front at her church. God had answered the desperate prayer of a young mom.

How do I know that God is real? Because while the medical community had deemed my Aunt's illness as hopeless, God responded with other plans for my Aunt. That was over 45 years ago, and my Aunt is still alive, still active in the church, and still very thankful that God is real and He still answers prayer.

You may not have such a phenomenal story to tell from your personal family, but there are many times you could point to in your life, instances where God gave you guidance or protection. Stories of how God became real to you through struggles you walked through in life exist and should be shared.

Telling your story is a powerful way of sharing Christ's love to those around you in life. On your upcoming trip, you will most likely have a chance to stand in front of people and share a story about what God has done in your life. In the back of this book, on pages: 113, 118 and 123, you will find helpful tips to develop your story. Your story is unique. It's worth telling, for you are a first-hand witness to God's forgiveness and Mercy. Proudly tell the world what God has done in your life!

Live It Out Loud – Serving Others

My last challenge for you to live out your faith is by serving others. Philippians 2:6 describes Jesus' servant heart, "Who, being in very nature God, did not consider equality with God something to be used to his own advantage; rather, he made himself nothing by taking the very nature of a servant, being made in human likeness. And being found in appearance as a man, he humbled himself by becoming obedient to death— even death on a cross!" Jesus influenced His world by what He said, but also by the example He set by serving people. Every time He was confronted with a problem of someone in need, He stopped whatever He was doing and served him or her and helped solve his or her issue. No issue was too big or small that He didn't take time to be part of the solution. What an amazing example for us to follow.

People who are great servants don't seem to grab the headlines, except for a few amazing people like Mother Teresa. Most avoid the spotlight so as not to be noticed. I had the privilege of knowing a man just like that; his name was Vern.

Vern was a retired bachelor in our church and he lived in a little one-room house. He was at church every time the doors were open and was always looking for ways to serve. If you lived in our town, you could have seen him driving his old International pick-up to the church very, very slowly to volunteer his work. In the summer time, he maintained an old Farmall Cub tractor with a mower deck from the church garage and could be seen cutting the several acres of grass on the church property several days a week. In the wintertime, Vern would drive out to the church every time a snowflake would fall and start to cumulate on the church sidewalks. When he wasn't outside working, he would volunteer his time in the office by folding bulletins and cleaning up the sanctuary after the weekly services. If something needed to be done, Vern would most likely be doing it before anyone had a chance to talk with others about possibly helping with the project – he had an amazing servants heart.

Vern hated receiving recognition for his servant's heart. I heard a story about Vern. It happened before my time on staff. The church thought it would be a great idea to publicly recognize Vern for his many hours of volunteering at the church so they ambushed him on a Sunday morning, and talked about him in front of the church, publicly thanking him for all the work he did around the building and presented him with a gift certificate to a local department store. I understand, Vern was greatly embarrassed by this public display of affection for him. He didn't feel like he deserved any praise for what he was doing to help the church function. Upon his death, it was a common belief that Vern never cashed that gift certificate at the store because it could be viewed as prideful and accepting praise from man vs. praise from God. Galatians 1:10 (NLT) says, "Obviously, I'm not trying to win the approval of people, but of God. If pleasing people were my goal, I would not be Christ's servant."

Vern had such a servant's heart, and it was a honor to call him a friend. I miss my time of sitting next to him in the office and listening to his many stories about his time on the railroad. I still marvel at his unwillingness to accept praise from man. What a pure heart he had; I wish I could have spent more time with him, more telling though, I wish that I could honestly say that I have a heart like Vern. There was a huge void at the church, the day Vern passed away and went on to receive his rewards in heaven. The world would be a much better place with more "guys like Vern," people that feel like their mission in life is to serve others in need. Do you have a servant's heart? Are you seeking the approval of people or of God?

My challenge to you is to Live It Out Loud. Establish prayer and reading the Bible as daily routines or habits, for those feed your personal relationship with Jesus Christ. I also want to challenge you to go public in your faith and be ready to share your story about what a difference Christ has made in your life. I Peter 3:15 says, "...Always be prepared to give an answer to everyone who asks you to give the reason for the hope that you have."

Many locked doors will be opened by a servant's heart! Use the time leading up to your trip to establish these daily routines in your life, for these habits will help you Live It Out Loud!

Chapter 3

Week #1

Devotionals

Stories from Mission Trip Veterans

Challenges for the Week:

Read One Devotional per day. Answer the questions in the Daily Watermark Challenge with more than a one-word answer, put some thought into your responses.

Read: 1 chapter of the Old Testament, 1 chapter of the New Testament, 1 Psalm and a Proverb each day.

Memorize:
Jeremiah 29:11 - For I know the plans I have for you, declares the Lord; plans to prosper you and not to harm you, plans to give you hope and a future.
Isaiah 53:5 - But he was pierced for our transgressions, he was crushed for our iniquities; the punishment that brought us peace was on him, and by his wounds we are healed.

Prayer. Take ten minutes or more, complete the revolving calendar, start praying for your team, trip leaders, and missionary or ministry host.

Develop your story: of what God has done in your life to share with family and friends. It can also be publicly shared on the trip.

Bobby
Trip Location: Edinburgh, Scotland
Occupation: Youth Alive - Home Missionary

Ministry highlights: Speaking in schools about choices, sharing my most important choic
in life - a relationship with Jesus Christ, and relating how that helps me daily, preaching at
youth rally, and visiting the Edinburgh Castle were especially memorable.

What I learned from the trip: It was my first real step of faith in raising money and sharin
my faith publicly. I was amazed at how much I grew from following Christ's leading an
going on this trip. My life has never been the same.

Proverbs 22:1 (NLT) Choose a good reputation over great riches; being held in high esteer
is better than silver or gold.

Live – Build A Reputation

I will never forget my first day of high school because it was a little rough. I wa
transferring from a very small private school with only a handful of students in my grade t
a new school with 768 other sophomores. The toughest part of the day was walking int
the lunchroom – seemingly about the size of a Wal-Mart parking lot - not knowing a singl
person. So, there I was, lunch tray in hand feeling stupid as I looked across the crowd fo
an open spot to eat my lunch. I wish I could tell you of the hero that walked up to me an
said "hey – you look new here, why don't you come sit with my friends and me at our table,
but sadly, no hero appeared that day.

As time went on, things became much easier, and I quickly picked up the flow of th
schedule. I did eventually make some friends, but I also realized I needed to take a stand o
some important things right away, like...was I a Ford or Chevy fan? Did I like heavy meta
music or was I more of a rap guy? Did I like sports or was I more into the arts? With eac
choice I displayed, I was determining which group I would soon attach myself to.

Looking back, I was really building a reputation. The choices and statements I mad
started to shape who I was as I walked the hallways of my school. Thankfully, I had a few
great friends that I could rely on to help me stay strong in my faith and stay consistent i
my witness as a follower of Jesus Christ.

It's not too late for you to build your reputation! You may have made some bad choices i
the past or became involved with the wrong crowd, but what you do from this day forwar
will really determine who you will be. I love this quote, "It's never too late to become th
person you were meant to be" (Mark Batterson). It's not too late for you to change who yo
are and become the influential person Jesus Christ has meant you to be on your schoo
campus!

For what traits are you known on your campus? What does your reputation say about you?

Do these characteristics make you proud? Why or why not?

If you could change one impression about your reputation on your campus, what would it be?

What are some ways you can immediately start building your reputation as a follower of Christ?

What is one step you can take today to start that process?

Quoting Mark Batterson, "It's never too late to become the person you were meant to be"...
      Who are you meant to be? Write a short paragraph describing what your life will look like ten years from now.

Sarah
Trip Location: Chiang Mai, Thailand
Occupation: Registered Nurse

Ministry highlights: I enjoyed going to Chiang Mai, Thailand, where our group hosted a English camp where we taught Sunday school lessons during our English lessons. W advertised on a local college campus for the English lessons, and our group also delivere the Book of Hope to homes in the area.

Mark 10:44-45 (NIV) And whoever wishes to be first among you shall be slave of all. Fo even the Son of Man did not come to be served, but to serve, and to give His life a ranson for many."

Serve

Thailand was my first mission trip, and it was an inspirational start. It was a life-changing event, especially with it being the summer before I started college. I learned how to serve and be patient and spread God's word despite a language barrier. Growing up, most of u think primarily of "me," but when God sends you on a missions trip, you learn it is no about "you;" it's about Him. This verse was the inspiration for the humbling experience had on my AIM trip. God taught me it wasn't about me. It was all about serving. As we embarked on the trip, it felt like we weren't really doing much. When you go on a missio trip, you want to feel like you are doing something and making a difference while bringing people to God. I learned that this is not always the case; sometimes, you just sow the see by serving and leave the missionaries you worked with to water and watch the growth. felt like I needed to do something and bring someone to Christ. In this sense, I was feeling like I had to be served. I was trying to serve myself by saying that I brought "umpteen people to Christ. Instead, we learned to serve.

We did everything our missionaries asked of us. We stamped books with their logos, we pu together bags with the Book of Hope to give to people, we delivered the bags to people who lived near the church, and we passed out flyers to students at the local college. I didn't fee like we really did anything on this trip, but at the end of the trip, the missionaries thanked us for everything we did and how we served the people. I thought about this for a while Through the actions of us being present and doing all these minor tasks that the missionaries needed done, I was serving. This life is about serving people and God, no about trying to feel self-gratified by being the "awesome Christian." By doing the tasks tha needed to be done and having a good attitude about them, we served and planted the seed and the missionaries were able to see the fruit of that.

Can you go out and serve someone in your community? Go and offer to serve them in any little task they might have. Do not think of what this will do for you, but just do it to serve others. Do some little things like volunteering to run those papers to the office for a teache or volunteer to do the laundry for your mom. You can make serving a daily habit in your life!

o I serve those in my life and community, or am I doing these things to serve myself?

ow can I serve those around me today with a good attitude while still being humble?

ow can I make serving a daily habit in my life? List five ideas.

o I serve only to be recognized by others? Or am I doing it for the right reasons (to serve ke Christ)?

Kathy
Trip Location: Panama City, Panama
Occupation: Physician Assistant

Ministry highlights: I have heard it said before that those going on a mission trip are impacted more than the people being served. I was overwhelmed to see how giving the people from Panama were. They were the ones who wanted to serve us and help us, from the wonderful meals they served, to opening their homes and giving their time. They were delighted to spend time with us. I especially saw this in the children; whether on the street or in a school, they were always so joyful and giving.

James 4:8 (NIV) Come near to God and he will come near to you.

Prayer

Prayer is essential to the Christian life. There are many seasons of life. Sometimes we think we have it together, but at other times it feels like we are spinning out of control. The sentiment from James 4:8 has permeated all aspects of my life. When I was in high school, loved God and tried to serve Him with all my heart; however, my worldview was limited to my family, friends, town, and maybe some special youth events. I wanted to know God on a deeper level, so I stepped outside my comfort zone to travel to Panama on a missions trip.

I thought it would be fun to see another part of the world and get to know other Christian youth. While I had these experiences, I also found that God opened my eyes and world view. Although the Panamanian Christians had few worldly possessions, the joy and peace they felt from Christ was evident. Some of the memories that have been embedded in my mind are the HUGE smiles and laughing. They were happy with little because it meant that they needed to rely on God and come near to Him even more. I remember the meals - always rice and chicken- and knowing that they were feeding us their limited chickens (we would see the chickens one day and then not the next). Rather than worrying about their future meals and lack of chickens, these gracious people put their trust in God. This intimate relationship can only be found from spending quality time with God through prayer.

Since that missions trip, there have been numerous seasons in my life. It still is my deepest desire to be in God's will. I want to come near to God and know Him intimately. I still remember the joy and peace from the people from Panama; this can only come from God. Recently, a speaker I heard stated that, "God wants to lead us more than we want to follow Him." We need to do our part of coming near to God. He is there and wants more than anything to come near to us.

ow can I draw closer to God today?

ow is my prayer life? Do I sincerely try to "come near to God" and seek His will for my life?

m I praying not only for the people who I am going to help on a mission's trip but also for ne ways I will be affected by this missions experience?

ow can I pray and reach out to those around me starting today?

Vhat are your present expectations regarding the culture and how they may worship here? After the trip review them.

Sarah
Trip Location: St. Petersburg, Russia
Occupation: Stay at Home Mom

Ministry highlights: Visiting an orphanage camp and playing with the children, as well going to the vendor markets and visiting the Winter Palace (a.k.a. the Heritage – largest art museum in the world), were amazing activities.

What I learned from the trip: No matter how others may look or where they come from God sees us all the same. No one person is more important than another.

1 Corinthians 16:14 (NLT) And everything you do must be done in love.

LIVE- Do EVERYTHING in Love!

Before going on my mission trip, people often asked me many questions about why I was going. Why did I want to fly half way around the world to help people I didn't know? Why did I feel it was so important to give up two weeks of my life to invest in others? My answer was simple: because Christ loved me, and in turn, I had a love for others. Not only did I have a love for others, but also I wanted them to know Christ and the amazing love he had for them.

The first duty of our trip was to paint a bedroom at an orphanage. Some may wonder how painting a bedroom for someone I would never meet was showing love. We weren't just painting a room; we were investing in someone's life. The children who lived in that room would know that someone loved them and cared enough about them to sacrifice their time and effort to make their day a little brighter. I didn't know how this might affect the children's future down the road. Could this be the one highlight they cling to and hold on to forever? Is this the one bright spot that keeps them going on days when they would rather stop? Knowing that someone flew thousands of miles just to paint a bedroom, a young boy or girl might be reminded of God's love. If a person they will never meet loved them enough to do something as simple as paint a room, how much more does God, who created them, love them!

We also spent time at a camp for orphans on our trip. We didn't speak the same language as the children at the camp, but in our love, we were able to communicate with them and share our lives with each other, if even just for that one day. We played games and tried to communicate by pointing or acting. We were able to laugh with them and love them, maybe like no one ever has. Even though we couldn't speak the same language or fully understand what the others were saying, we were able to show love through our actions. We showed them that we didn't care about social status or how much money they had. We didn't care what their background was or where they would be in a few years. We cared about sharing Christ and His love with them. We wanted to let them know that there was someone out there who cared more for them than we ever could. Christ loved them with an everlasting love and wants to know them personally!

e showed those children love, and we hoped that by showing them Christ's love, they ould come to know Him in a personal way. I believe that by showing love in this way, we anted a seed in the hearts of these children so they might get closer to knowing Jesus!

e must love those around us, just as Christ loves us. Sometimes it's easy to love those at live far away that we have an encounter with for two weeks, but what about those we e every day? We must also love them. It can be a lot harder, but that is what we have en called to do.

Daily Watermark Challenge

ow can you show love to those around you every day? (Parents, siblings, peers)

ven in situations when you don't speak the same language or you think you have nothing common, how can you show love to others?

ow would your actions differ if you did everything in love? In turn, how would others eact to you?

sus showed those around Him that He loved them by meeting their immediate needs? low can you do the same for the individuals you meet?

everything you do, say, or think is done with love, how do you think your outlook on the orld would change?

Mark
Trip Locations: Stockholm, Sweden, and Mexico City, Mexico.
Occupation: College student - Engineering

Ministry highlights: Performing human videos, fellowshipping with believers from a different culture, serving and witnessing to the lost, leading worship, and visiting the Mayan temples in Mexico and the Royal Palace in Stockholm have impacted me to this day.

1 Peter 4:10 (NIV) Each one should use whatever gift he has received to serve others, faithfully administering God's grace in its various forms.

Serve – God Gave You Gifts

As a sixteen-year-old thinking about going on my first mission's trip, I have to say, I was quite nervous. Many factors contributed to my apprehension, including, the thought of leaving the country without my family for the first time, unfamiliarity of the native language of the land – this may sound silly – the apprehension I felt about foreign food. The thought of not eating anything tasty didn't sound very appetizing to me (pun intended). However, the one thought that worried me the most was that, I did not know how I could contribute to the team. I didn't believe I had the skill set to serve others as I thought missionaries were supposed to. There are people who feel completely in their comfort zone talking to random strangers. In fact, they take joy in it. I am not one of those people. One on-one interactions with strangers always leave me feeling awkward and speechless. On top of that, when I try to give a speech or just talk in front of a crowd, I can literally feel my body heat rise. My face gets as red as a tomato and within two minutes my armpits are soaked.

So, why am I telling you all of this, you may ask. Well, I am just trying to emphasis the fact that I felt like I had nothing to offer my team. I couldn't give compelling testimonies, I didn't feel like much of a leader, I didn't have any creative ideas for human videos, and simply put, I just wasn't very good at talking. That's when I stumbled upon 1 Peter 4:1. I began to analyze what talents God had given me and how I could use those talents to serve others. That's when I realized I could do something with music.

I decided to try to use my gift of music to serve others. As it turned out, on both of my mission trips, I was able to be on a worship team. Leading worship was how God was able to work through me to reach others. I never used to think of leading worship as serving others, but after taking the words of 1 Peter to heart, I now realize that serving others has many different faces.

1 Peter 4:10 says God has given each one of us a gift to be used to serve His kingdom. It does not say God has given some people a gift to be used for His kingdom. I was trying to have the same talents I thought missionaries were supposed to have. This verse opened my eyes to see that everyone's gifts look different, and God made us like that on purpose in order to administer God's grace in its various forms.

When you normally think of ministry, what talents or skills apply directly?

Even though you may not have the talents you just listed above, <u>you have talents from God</u>. Take some time and think about your gifts.

How can you use your talents to serve others while benefitting His kingdom?

Is there anything holding you back from accepting God's call to serve others with your gifts?

What would be the next step you need to take in order to get your talent/gift "plugged in"?

Lukas
Trip Location: Panama City, Panama; Antigua, Guatemala
Occupation: College student

Ministry highlights: Sharing my story with students in schools and on the soccer field. Showing Christ's love and character through the sport of soccer, and creating close friendships with fellow team members have impacted me tremendously.

What I learned from the trip: Missions trips are not an inexpensive endeavor, so it was my first time really trusting God to help with my finances. He is good, and it was amazing to see Him provide in a variety of ways. Also, since my family was going through some extreme medical concerns during my trips, my financial concerns were heightened. It was cool to see Him use my story to reach some unexpected people.

Luke 12:22-25(NIV) Therefore I tell you, do not worry about your life...Who of you by worrying can add a single hour to his life?

Pray

Have you ever worried about something in your life? Maybe it was the test you had to pass in order to complete eighth grade, or it may have been a project assigned two months prior that you remembered the night before it was due. As I look back, I have come to realize that in every stressful situation I have ever encountered, Jesus has never let me down or left my side.

When I was in third grade, we had weekly spelling tests. One week, I aced my Monday test and was given ten complex words to study for Wednesday. The words were the names of dinosaurs, and almost all were relatively easy, all but one, that is. The word was Tyrannosaurus-Rex, and it ruined my Tuesday night. From my eyes flowed tears of frustration as I continuously spelled the word incorrectly. What seems like a minor problem now was insurmountable to me and my third grade self.

I have spent an awful amount of time worrying in my life. I've worried about my friends, my grades in school, and my future college. I've worried about first impressions, first dates, and first employers. One of my biggest worries has been wondering what God's plan is for my life. Am I following the right path? There have been negligible reasons to worry, but I've also experienced situations where worrying seems appropriate. Nevertheless, God doesn't want us to worry about the ample tasks, and he certainly doesn't want us to overemphasize the trivial matters in our days. God desires for us to cast all of our cares unto Him.

When we worry, we sometimes act as if God doesn't understand our situation. We put our trust in human, problem-solving abilities instead of believing in our loving, omnipotent father in heaven. It is not wrong to be concerned over an issue, but when we let those emotions take priority over our faith in God, our spiritual life will languish. Our God is a God who provides. God supplies resources when we trust Him with our finances. He provides healing when we believe in the miraculous. There is absolutely nothing our God can't do. We cannot allow worry to constrict our faith. So cast your cares unto Him, believe that He is for you, and live the stress-free life God intends for you!

Daily Watermark Challenge

How do you think a worry-free life would help your faith and relationship with Christ?

What are some issues that are hindering your trust with God?

What is something that you worry about too much?

What steps can you follow in order to worry less and trust God more?

Who is a leader/adult you trust who will help you in that process?

Week in review

Which devotional was most challenging to you this week, and why?

What is one thing God has challenged you to do this week? What's your plan to change

Describe how you have grown in your relationship with the Lord this week.

Chapter 4

Week #2
Devotionals
Stories from Mission Trip Veterans

Challenges for the Week:

Read One Devotional per day. Answer the questions in the Daily Watermark Challenge with more than a one-word answer, put some thought into your responses.

Read: 2 chapters of the Old Testament, 2 chapters of the New Testament, 2 Psalms and a Proverb each day.

Memorize:
Philippians 4:6-8
Do not be anxious about anything, but in every situation, by prayer and petition, with thanksgiving, present your requests to God. And the peace of God, which transcends all understanding, will guard your hearts and your minds in Christ Jesus. Finally, brothers and sisters, whatever is true, whatever is noble, whatever is right, whatever is pure, whatever is lovely, whatever is admirable - if anything is excellent or praiseworthy—think about such things.
John 3:16
For God so loved the world that He gave His one and only Son that whoever believes in Him will be saved.

Prayer. Take ten minutes or more, daily pray for items on the revolving calendar, continue to pray for your team, and leaders. Pray for favor with the Nationals, pastors.

Develop your story: Brainstorm and write down ideas of ways God has been real to you.

Steve
Trip location: Long Island, Bahamas
Occupation: Junior High Principal

Ministry highlights: I had the opportunity to share my testimony publicly for the first time. As a team, we had the opportunity to share the Gospel with elementary students at the local public school. Also, we shared the Gospel and prayed with the local people of the island. I had never lived out my faith so publicly.

Philippians 2:3-4 (NIV) Do nothing out of selfish ambition or vain conceit. Rather, in humility value others above yourselves, not looking to your own interests but each of you to the interests of the others.

Serve – Jesus, Others, You

As a 17 year old, I had the opportunity to join other youth from around the state of Minnesota on an AIM trip to Long Island, Bahamas. The trip held a lot of appeal for me. As a kid growing up in a rural community in Southern Minnesota, I had not experienced much of the world outside of my home state. The thought of serving God in a foreign country and visiting the ocean for the first time was too great to resist. I signed up expecting a great time in the sun but what I experienced was an amazing move of God that would shape who I am and give me a direction for my life.

God used me on this missions trip to not only share His word with others but to also show me a glimpse of my future. For the first time in my life, I was personally interacting with children and adults who were a different race and culture than me. I had spent my whole life interacting with people who looked just like me. For the first time, I was feeling the Holy Spirit leading me to live my life more intentionally amongst people who were not just like me. I was being called to serve, love, and share my faith with them.

After this trip, I moved to a major urban city in Minnesota to attend college. After college, intentionally started teaching and living in the poorest community of the city. God opened the doors for me to live and share my faith with my friends, neighbors, and former students. He taught me how to serve, love, and share my faith with people who were different from me but lived in my own neighborhood. The passion that God had lit inside me as a 17 year old is still burning brightly in me as an adult.

God recently moved me to a new city. After ten years as a middle school teacher, I am now serving as a principal in an ethnically and economically diverse junior high school. Daily, get to live my life and faith out, serving the youth and families of my community. I feel blessed to be able to serve God and my community in this capacity. Every day in this new job, I am forced to seek after God so that I may truly show Christ's love through my interactions with students and families. This is the path of service to others is the path that God placed me on as a 17 year old kid while experiencing God in a very real way on a missions trip in the Bahamas.

hink about a way that God can use you to serve others at your school or in your ommunity.

reak through your comfort zone to experience how God can use you to serve others.

eek out an opportunity to serve others in a multicultural setting.

how Christ's love anonymously by doing something good for someone.

olunteer your time or resources to a Christian organization that supports struggling amilies.

ntentionally spend time in prayer for an economically disadvantaged community.

Sarah
Trip Locations: Bahamas, Guatemala, Chile, and Nicaragua
Occupation: Employment Coordinator at a local non-profit organization

Ministry highlights: Culture and helping others are my passions, so naturally my favorit
parts of trips were working with the locals and helping in any way they needed! One of m
treasured memories is making tortillas with Guatemalan women in a small, hot, dirt-floo
kitchen. We laughed and worked together to create a delicious lunch for the team (and
only dropped two tortillas)!

II Corinthians 9:6-8 (NIV) Remember this: Whoever sows sparingly will also reap sparingl
and whoever sows generously will also reap generously. Each of you should give what yo
have decided in your heart to give, not reluctantly or under compulsion, for God loves
cheerful giver. And God is able to bless you abundantly, so that in all things at all time:
having all that you need, you will abound in every good work.

Giving Is Fun

"Giving away $315 is our pleasure."
What??!! Why would giving your money to me make *you* happy?!
I felt shocked then humbled at the generous gift. I knew the donors truly meant it, and
could imagine their smiling faces as they made the decision to bless me in this way.
thought of other true stories of people cheerfully giving to others: a young woma
anonymously sending $1000 each to four missionaries she knew personally; a perso
donating $1000 for siblings to go on a missions trip; a man literally emptying his wallet at
church service; a couple willing to buy a plane ticket - on the condition they remai
anonymous - for a college student to visit her sick mother; a short-term missionar
receiving a check for the exact amount she had left to raise; a small congregation donatin
$1400 in one offering to help earthquake and tsunami relief ministry in Japan. I saw thes
generous donations from people who were truly joyful to give their money away. Thes
examples inspire and challenge me to give with a cheerful heart, even as I wonder wha
difference my measly few dollars can make. Our gifts don't have to be big or dramatic; w
don't have to necessarily empty our pockets in order to serve God. A cheerful, willing hear
and obedience is what God loves, whether it's $5 or $500.

When I was a college student, a speaker shared a message in chapel about developing a
habit of giving. An offering plate passed through the audience, and we were encouraged t
add something to the plate. It didn't have to be money necessarily, but the speake
challenged each of us to give something. As the plate passed, I could see a paperclip, a pen
a piece of scratch paper, a piece of gum, along with coins and dollar bills. We were buildin
a habit of giving. That message stayed with me, and years later I'm still trying to exhibi
this, though, I admit, some times are easier than others to give.

You've probably never regretted being generous. It's more likely the opposite: after giving
you felt a deep joy or contentment. We can't take a single tangible thing with us when w
die, but here on earth we can give money to missions and invest in eternal souls.

Just imagine the stories we'll hear and the people we'll meet in heaven that are there because of the money we cheerfully gave! That is exciting, and nothing is a better investment.

Daily Watermark Challenge

List examples of giving you've heard of or experienced?

What's your current attitude about giving?

What are some ways God is asking you to give?

What are your challenges or hesitancies of being generous?

List one or two ways you'll practice the habit of giving in the next two weeks?

Kelly
Trip location: Panama, Guatemala
Occupation: Social worker

Ministry Highlights: Going to schools and orphanages to speak with youth and children about Jesus and how He has had the biggest impact on my life were life changing. I was able to share my testimony about how having Jesus in my heart has helped me each and every day of my life. I also loved spending time with the people from the churches and in the community with those who were eager to hear about the Lord.

What I learned from this trip: I learned that God is powerful, and trusting Him is something I will never regret. I learned that even though we don't all speak the same language, the language of the Lord is universal, and everyone, everywhere is hungry for what He can do.

Philippians 4:6 (NIV) Do not be anxious about anything, but in everything, by prayer and petition, with thanksgiving, present your requests to God.

Prayer

My first mission trip was to Panama. We were supposed to go to Guatemala, but because of unrest in the country, we went to Panama instead. From early on, I was certain there was no way I would be able to make this trip a reality. My family did not have much money, and I knew that each and every cent would have to be raised in order for me to go. The anxiety that I felt about being able to do what God had asked me to do was so real. I felt much anticipation and could not wait until it was time to go and experience everything that I had heard so much about from those who went on mission trips before me. I found myself nervous and almost paralyzed at times. I was fearful of what would happen while I was there and about how I would be able to raise the money to go and do all God wanted me to do.

From the planning stages of this trip, I was encouraged to go to God's word and trust what it was telling me. I worked hard to make praying a daily habit. This was a difficult endeavor at times. My family was going through a lot of stress at the time, and I was not entirely sure that God could hear me when I prayed. I know God heard each and every word I was praying. Needless to say, I went on this trip and even went on another one the following year. Proving that God provided all I needed for this trip. He made it possible for me to raise all the money I needed as well as ready my heart to make a difference for those who were so hungry to hear about God. This, in turn, made a difference in my heart.

While in Panama, I was reminded regularly about the power of prayer. Taking time each day to be with God has been my saving grace. It has been the glue that has kept me strong through many struggles and many joys. I am so grateful for creating a habit of prayer because now it is just part of my day, and it has never failed me.

What is one obstacle that gets in the way of making prayer a daily habit in your life?

If you knew that praying regularly could change your course for good, what would it take to make it happen?

What positive outcomes have come for you from praying?

Could you commit to praying for a few minutes every day for 30 days to help make prayer a daily habit for you?

Can you think of a time when you did not trust God by going to prayer and how that impacted the outcome?

Matt
Trip Location: Hurricane Katrina Disaster Relief in New Orleans
Occupation: Insurance Agent

Ministry highlights: Life can be changed in a blink of an eye, and I truly felt this as I traveled from an American city to what felt like a third world country just by driving to another state. It was very cool to see Graceland on the way back home.

What I learned from this trip: The one lesson I'll take away from the trip is how quickly things can be destroyed. We were cleaning out this house that had been abandoned so it could be demolished. The house still looked like someone lived there; the table was set and clothes were still in the dresser. They still had the fancy china in cupboard; it was kind of an eerie feeling since the walls in the house were so soft that you could push your finger right through them.

Matthew 6:19-20 (NIV) Do not store up for yourselves treasures on earth, where moth and rust destroy, and where thieves break in and steal. But store up for yourselves treasures in heaven, where moth and rust do not destroy, and where thieves do not break in and steal.

Live - Focus on God, Not Things

It was back in 2005 that Hurricane Katrina struck the Gulf Coast creating much destruction in its path. So, my youth pastor put together a team, and off we went on a twenty-five hour nonstop drive to help out the city of New Orleans. To this day, I can still remember walking for blocks in the ninth ward where the levy broke and seeing where houses once stood. It was mindboggling cleaning out a church, only to see the fully armed National Guard drive past. They were carrying machine guns and wearing body armor, and they were driving around in a Humvee. Added air support was evident by the countless Black Hawk helicopters flying overhead. I remember my pastor asked a couple of the Guardsmen what they were doing, and I was shocked to learn they were protecting us.

Seeing how in a blink of an eye that everything you have and cherish can be destroyed, I have to continue to ask myself what I treasure most. Is it the things of this world that can be destroyed or stolen? Instead, it is the treasures that will be stored up in heaven; like standing up for the kid being bullied in school, or helping out the family you know that is going through a tough time, or how about doing something without any thought of getting anything in return.

I believe God wants us to be blessed, but He doesn't want us to put a higher priority on material belongings over what is truly important – loving God and loving people.

To see where you put your treasure: do you look to always have the newest and nicest possessions, or do you look to always help the homeless, hungry, and the sick?

f your house was about to be destroyed, and you could save only one item, what it be and explain why?

What are some ways you could help others who have experienced loss?

Brainstorm ideas of how you can be a blessing to someone who has experienced tragedy.

Holly

Trip location: Long Island, Bahamas

Occupation: Assistant Professor of New Testament at Westmont College in Santa Barbara, California.

Ministry highlights: Besides the obvious highlight of a Bahamian beach with clear turquoise water, I remember walking in groups to visit residents of the island. It was so awkward at times but so powerful! Many of the people we invited came to our evening services, and the Spirit of God transformed lives!

Matthew 6:9-13 (CEB) Pray like this: Our Father who is in heaven, uphold the holiness of your name. Bring in your kingdom so that your will is done on earth as it's done in heaven. Give us the bread we need for today. Forgive us for the ways we have wronged you, just as we also forgive those who have wronged us. And don't lead us into temptation, but rescue us from the evil one.

Pray – Scripture

Thanks to good teaching and modeling from my parents, I have always been comfortable praying, both silently and out loud. Going on a mission trip, though, stretched my prayers even more. Praying in a different place, a place with so many needs, made the need to pray more real. I remember being there, looking around, and thinking, "How do I pray for this? What do I say?" Have you ever felt that way?

Of course, Jesus taught his followers how to pray, and sometimes we need to go back to the Lord's prayer and remind ourselves of what Jesus cares about. I think that the Common English Bible translation really brings out the power of the passage, and I encourage the students in my New Testament classes to use it as a guide. I now pray this way: "God, uphold your holiness. Prove to this place, and everyone here, who You are. Let us see You. (v. 9). Bring Your kingdom! Come on, God! Please fix what is wrong with the world so that our world matches what You care about (v. 10). Give everyone enough to eat; this is your heart (v. 11). Help us to forgive on this trip and in our lives because that is what You do for us (v. 12). And protect us, as we participate in what You are already doing in this place. Be with us! We need You (v. 13)!"

I recently participated in a "walk for water" campaign; it was a fundraiser to provide clean water for kids in the Democratic Republic of Congo. I cried when I heard about these kids who get sick, and even die, because they don't have clean water to drink. My kids have clean water to drink (and milk and juice too!). As I was walking, I was praying for God to fix this because when God is king, God fixes what is wrong with the world (like dirty water) But God wants to use us, the church, to help fix the world too! What a challenge to participate in what God is doing!

Pray "bigger." The Lord's prayer invites us, challenges us, to do that! It is always good practice for us to remember as 21st Century North Americans that God's world is bigger than our country, and AIM trips help us to experience that.

ke your cues from the Lord's Prayer and ask God to prove to the world who He is and at He cares about. Ask God to fix, restore, and provide in ways that only He can. Ask God help you and protect you and use you and your team! Pray like Jesus taught us to pray. ien!

Daily Watermark Challenge

r what do you typically pray? How often are you praying for yourself?

w does the Lord's Prayer challenge you to pray "bigger?"

Jesus taught us to pray this way, what does this mean for the importance of this prayer?

hat would it look like for you to pray "bigger", both at home and on your trip?

hat kinds of things would you ask God to do?

Travis
Trip Location: Quetzaltenango, Guatemala
Occupation: US Army Special Forces

Ministry highlights: Going to the Guatemalan prisons and tuberculosis hospitals to minister to the people left a huge impression on me.

What I learned from the trip: More than anything I realized how much God has blessed us in America and how we need to thank Him daily for the opportunities and gifts He gives us

Psalms 91:15 (AMP) He shall call upon me, and I will answer Him; I will be with him in trouble, I will deliver Him and honor Him.

Pray

I currently serve in the US Army, and I am a veteran of Operation Iraqi Freedom. In the summer of 2005, we were at a forward operating base far in the northwest part of Iraq. Our higher headquarters (HQ) was on a different base about two and a half hours by vehicle from our location. We had received orders from our commander to drive to the location of our HQs in order to speak with a high-ranking US Army official about some insignificant issues and to have a BBQ; these orders were not received with enthusiasm. Driving to the other base would take us down numerous dangerous roads and would include driving through Tal-Afar, a hotbed of insurgent activity. To me, the risk of driving to the other location was ridiculous; in my opinion, the risk was not worth the reward.

As I climbed into the gunner's position in the truck, I was quietly grumbling to myself, "Why do we have to drive to this location, just to talk to some guy?" "What if someone gets hurt or something happens; it will be for nothing." I went on and on in my head, fostering a poor attitude. Then, from God the most audible voice I have ever heard resounded. God said: "Quit complaining! I don't need a war to take you home!" Everything in me was silent; I could not believe what I had just heard. In that moment God reminded me that He was in control. It did not matter how many bullets were fired or how big an improvised explosive device was, nothing that could touch me without His consent.

The rest of that deployment, I made a conscious effort to remember that God does control what happens. I also promised to be a better witness. We may not like what happens or understand it when it does, but no matter what, He is in control.

If something in your life seems to be falling down around you, spend time in quiet prayer to figure what God is trying to teach you through the hardship. Just as a parent uses difficult circumstances to teach his / her children about life, so does the Heavenly Father use life's difficulties to bring us closer to Him.

I had a very close friend on my team who died in Iraq in 2004. Like many others, our vehicle was hit with an explosive device, and despite our best efforts, he lost his life. His parents were Christians, and at the funeral they said something to my wife I will never

rget. Once they saw her, they gave her a big hug and they told her that at first they had
ard that everyone in the truck had died, but they were so glad that it was ONLY their
n. The ability to have peace in difficult times and to say something like that is
pernatural and can only come from one place.

Daily Watermark Challenge

ave you ever felt God's direction or heard God's voice? If you followed it, or not, what was
e end result?

any times we worry not about God's inability to handle our situation, but that his plan
n't our plan. Think back to a time where God's plan wasn't your plan. What was the end
sult?

you are currently going through difficult times, examine yourself. Is there sin in your life
od is trying to expel, or is God trying to encourage growth and dependence on Him?

as there ever been a time when your witness to others was damaged because of your lack
f faith?

Week in review

Which devotional was most challenging to you this week, and why?

What is one thing God has challenged you to do this week? What's your plan to change

Describe how you have grown in your relationship with the Lord this week.

Chapter 5

Week #3
Devotionals
Stories from Mission Trip Veterans

Challenges for the Week:

Read One Devotional per day. Answer the questions in the Daily Watermark Challenge with more than a one-word answer, put some thought into your responses.

Read: 2 chapters of the Old Testament, 2 chapters of the New Testament, 2 Psalms and a Proverb each day.

Memorize:
Matthew 28:19-20
Therefore go and make disciples of all nations, baptizing them in the name of the Father and of the Son and of the Holy Spirit, and teaching them to obey everything I have commanded you. And surely I am with you always, to the very end of the age.
Proverbs 3:5–6
Trust in the Lord with all your heart and lean not on your own understanding; in all your ways submit to him, and he will make your paths straight.

Prayer. Take ten minutes or more; pray through the revolving calendar, pray for your team, safety on the trip, for finances, for details of the trip.

Develop your story: Start to write out your story, ask your coach to help you select a story that tells how God has been at work in your life.

Jess
Trip locations: St. Petersburg, Russia, and Dillingham, Alaska
Occupation: Clinical Pharmacist

Ministry highlights: Realizing the impact of other people's sacrificial giving to support missionaries and how crucial that is for continued ministry were influential experiences. Giving had always been something God had placed on my heart but actually seeing it at work left a lifelong impression on me.

Proverbs 11:24 (ESV) One gives freely, yet grows all the richer; another withholds what he should give, and only suffers want.

Give—Prepare Yourself To Be Used by God

Waiting until you have time to volunteer or money to spare will only guarantee one thing i your life, it won't happen. In today's society, people are being pulled in countless direction from a young age. Because of our culture, it is important to set priorities early in life.

Something that I have slowly been learning is to actively leave room in my schedule and i my budget to allow God to use me in a big way. If we view time, talents, and money a personal property, it is harder to let God have free reign in our lives. I remind myself on regular basis that my talents, income, and my schedule fully belong to God, and He has th final say of how it is used.

One practical way I do this is while I am preparing to go on a mission trip is by purposefull setting aside a portion of money, trusting God is going to give me direction on how to use i during the trip. By doing this, God has used me to purchase medicines for patients, bu new kitchen utensils for one of our host cooks, buy bus fares for strangers, and be a answer to prayer for acute needs of my new friends around the world. I continue to liv with that mindset in my day to day life, and God has used me to send kids to camp, bu groceries for people, and volunteer at church and free medical clinics as well as countless other opportunities.

Knowing that you are being used by God to practically meet the needs of others i energizing and fulfilling, whether it is through giving money and gifts or just having the time to be there for friends and help out in your local community. It is also a contagiou way to live as a Christian. As you start to give more areas of your life to God, you realize how He can do so much more with what He's given you than you ever could. It inspires you to give it all to Him!

Always leave room in your budget and schedule for the Holy Spirit to use you in a radica way. Work at establishing a lifestyle that enables you to give to others when you feel God prompting you. I promise you will be rewarded ten times over for your preparation to be used by God!

God prompted you to give ten hours a week for Him above and beyond what you are giving right now, would you have the time to give? If not, what could you give up?

hen was the last time God unexpectedly used you, and how did you feel afterwards?

ow are you actively preparing to be used by God?

hat are some ways you can begin to support missionaries around the world?

hink of a time when someone else sacrificed his or her time or money for you. How did is make you feel, and how did you respond?

Rachel
Trip Location: Santo Domingo, Dominican Republic
Occupation: Registered Nurse

Ministry highlights: praying with children and families, playing with the children, seeing God work through serving Him, and seeing the joy in the hearts of changed lives created lifelong memories.

What I learned from the trip: God can use me whether I am serving him overseas or in my day-to-day mission field of life. Knowing this has brought me abundant opportunities in my life to share God's love and truth with those around me.

Psalm 27:23 (NLT) The Lord directs the steps of the godly. He delights in every detail of their lives.

SERVE: God Can Even Use You!

Serving God can take on a whole new meaning in life when you realize God can even use YOU in your everyday life. For a while, I grew up thinking that God could only really work through you if you became a missionary in a foreign land, a pastor, or leader of some Christian organization or church ministry. After experiencing my first overseas mission trip, God really opened my eyes to see how I could serve and be used by Him not only overseas, but each day of my life wherever He leads. I remember returning from the Dominican Republic with a bigger heart and a desire to serve people in need. I began praying every day that God would direct my steps and lead me to serve for His glory. He began to show and use me to serve those around me in need.

God knows you and has created you to serve in a way like no one else. It doesn't matter if you find yourself on the streets of the Dominican Republic, in the cubicle of some company, in a dorm room, at the local hospital, in the company of a friend, or in the midst of a classroom full of students. God can even use YOU because your mission field is wherever God has placed you at any given time. When you are serving others, you are serving God. Every morning you awaken, realize that as a child of God you are serving Him in whatever you are doing - big or small. Expect God to do great things and open your eyes to the needs around you.

Pray before you start each day and ask God to direct your steps and lead you to serve others in whatever your day may bring.

ow can I serve someone today? What gifts or talents has God given me to serve others?

here is God directing and motivating me to serve?

ho is in need around me, and how can I show them God's love?

ow can I be a better servant of Christ? How is God using me in my every day life?

Will
Trip location: New Orleans, Hurricane Katrina/Rita Response
Occupation: Youth Pastor

Ministry highlights: Responding to an internationally known disaster (a part of history gaining a new perspective of what serving looks like, and gaining a new appreciation fo the blessings I had were of utmost value to me.

Philippians 2:1-4 (NIV) Therefore if you have any encouragement from being united wit Christ, if any comfort from his love, if any common sharing in the Spirit, if any tendernes and compassion, then make my joy complete by being like-minded, having the same love being one in spirit and of one mind. Do nothing out of selfish ambition or vain concei Rather, in humility value others above yourselves, not looking to your own interests bu each of you to the interests of the others.

Serve

When I went to New Orleans to respond to the need created by the destruction o Hurricanes Katrina and Rita, many tasks needed attention. Roofs needed temporary blu tarps so they would not leak, people needed to be fed, and land needed to be cleared s temporary housing could be constructed. I was in a group of eager teenagers ready an willing to do anything asked of us, or so we thought.

After enduring two hard days of work. I was able to help cover some houses with tarp serve food to people in need, and clear land for FEMA trailers to be delivered. On th morning of the third day, we were assigned jobs. The leader of the organization that hoste us had left and put someone else in charge. He found out that most of us were not 18 an because of our age, he thought we couldn't do the same work we had been doing. Ou assignment for that day was to clean out and organize two closets in the building where w were staying.

My group and I had bad attitudes all day. We had driven many, many hours in a cramme van to help people in need, not to organize office supplies. We were upset and did not pu forth a good effort in work that day. We wanted to return home, even though we had a few days left in our trip.

That night, our youth leader gave us a great lesson in humility. We realized that our heart wanted assignments that were cool, so we could hang an invisible medal around our neck saying, "I cleaned up after a hurricane." Our ambition was about our status; our desire wa about us looking like saints, yet our attitudes that day were far from saintly.

This trip wasn't about us; it was about helping others. It wasn't about us being comfortable it was about making sure those affected by the hurricane could experience a little more comfort. The lesson learned from that day is when you serve, you serve others and th interests of others above yourself. Whatever you are asked to do, do it with the same love Spirit, and mind of Christ.

Serving isn't about what "I" want; it's about what "you" need.

Daily Watermark Challenge

nd a way to serve someone today – mow somebody's lawn, make someone dinner, watch meone's kids. Do these tasks for free.

heck your attitude – Think about the areas you serve others. How is your attitude? Are u happy to help or do you dread doing it? The next time you serve, do it not for your own terest but for the interests of the person/organization you are serving.

ray – Pray that you could have the same love, heart, and mind as Jesus. Also, pray that you e the opportunities in front of you to serve others. Realize the countless opportunities in ont of you.

Kelsey
Trip Location: Panama City, Panama
Occupation: College Student

Ministry highlights: We went into schools and promoted an event for girls. This event was focused on being created in the image of God. We were able to spread God's love to all the students through videos, testimonies, human videos, and games. I had the opportunity to share my testimony, which fit in with the topic of the event we were promoting.

What I learned from the trip: I learned to let go of what was holding me back from living out God's will in my life. My focus in life was shifted from myself to pleasing God in everything I do. Also, I learned not to be afraid of what people thought of me. Through this, I am now able to tell people who I really am.

Matthew 5:48 (NIV) Therefore you are to be perfect, as your heavenly Father is perfect.

Live - What's Holding You back?

Throughout my life, I have struggled with my self-esteem. Consistently, I compared myself to other girls, whether I knew them personally or they were in the media. I did not feel "perfect." I felt as though I could never live up to anyone's expectations. I was never good enough. I was never the best. I was never the prettiest, the smartest, the most athletic, or the most musical. It was difficult for me to see my strengths and my talents. Because of the unrealistic expectations I set for myself, I struggled on a daily basis to see the wonderful being God created in me.

One day, I read a verse during my devotions and it changed my life. The verse was Song of Songs 4:7 (NIV), "All beautiful you are, my darling; there is no flaw in you." I live by this verse now. Every time I have a thought that I am not beautiful or not good enough, I repeat this verse to myself. Even though I do have flaws and I am nowhere near perfect, God created me and loved me in a way that I could be flawless through Him. God has wiped all my flaws and sins, and I am perfectly created.

I want to encourage you. I am not sure what might be holding you back from completely loving yourself, but give it to God. Do everything you do with your whole heart. Every day do your best not to focus on yourself but focus on God. Be humble. Every day in your school, you are a light in a dark place. You are representing God by your actions and attitude. If you are constantly tearing yourself apart, people will see that. Be an example. Be a *Godly* example. If you have confidence in yourself, others will see that. God calls us to love everyone, even our enemies. You must be able to love yourself before you can love anyone else fully. It doesn't matter if you aren't the best. God created you the way you are, and you are perfect in His eyes. So, live out who God wants you to be, and He will love you for who you are.

What can you do to not to focus on yourself and earthly things? Instead, what can you do to live for God with your whole heart?

What is holding you back from loving God and others with your whole heart?

What is holding you back from loving who you are?

What are some expectations that you are putting on yourself that are not uplifting to yourself?

What are some ways you can tell people your story but still be yourself around them?

Julie
Trip Location: St. Petersburg, Russia
Occupation: Domestic Engineer (a.k.a. stay-at-home mom), married to a pastor

Ministry highlights: Seeing the amazing architecture and works of art in The Hermitage, working in an orphanage and at the campground, and spending time in prayer as a group made an incredible impression upon me.

What I learned from the trip: There are lost people all around me. Sometimes it's easy to become complacent and forget how much people need to know Jesus. Our hearts should ache for the lost, and I need to pray daily that God gives me the kind of compassion Jesus has for people.

Matt. 9:35-36 (NIV) Jesus went through all the towns and villages, teaching in their synagogues, proclaiming the good news of the kingdom and healing every disease and sickness. When he saw the crowds, he had compassion on them, because they were harassed and helpless, like sheep without a shepherd.

Pray

When I went to Russia, I had already been on three mission trips around the world. I was a seasoned pro or so I thought. But God used that trip to teach me what it really meant to have compassion. I found Russia to be the most depressing place I had ever visited. No one smiled at us on the subway. People didn't say hello. They avoided eye contact - not just with us, but also with everyone. They all went about their lives looking hopeless. It gave me the overall impression that Russia was a very dark, unhappy place to live.

One night, our group had gathered together to pray for the Russian people, and God broke my heart, showing me how lost they were. I became overwhelmed with emotion, thinking about all trials they've experienced throughout history (war, revolution, communism, oppression, corruption, poverty) and the state they're in now. I started crying uncontrollably as I prayed, and soon I couldn't even formulate words. I could feel their hopelessness, fear, and depression, and it made me feel physically ill.

The word "compassion" used here, when translated from the original Greek language (σπλαγχνίζομαι, pronounced like "splahg-neet-zo-my"), literally means that Jesus' guts churned. Jesus was looking at the people around Him, and He was overwhelmed with emotion for these people who were lost. Have you ever heard or seen something so sad it made you sick to your stomach or your heart actually ache? That's the kind of emotional reaction that Jesus felt.

Just like the crowd Jesus observed, the people I saw in Russia were sheep without a shepherd. Without a place in which to put their hope, they were lost.

re you seeing the lost people around you? Does it break your heart? Pray that God makes ur gut churn for those that don't know Him yet.

preparing for your trip, pray for those you will be ministering to - that you would be uly moved with compassion for them.

re there particular areas of your life where you've become hard-hearted and apathetic?

re there certain people that God has laid on your heart to pray for? Or has He called you to ray for specific people groups?

ow do you think God wants to use you to reach them?

Riley
Trip Location: Antigua, Guatemala
Occupation: High School Student

Ministry highlights - Playing soccer and speaking at halftime to the fans and the opposin
team. Cleaning up the local soccer team's soccer field, and watching Lionel Messi score
hat trick against the Guatemalan national soccer team will be lifelong memories from m
mission trip.

What I learned from the trip: I realized that I am so lucky to have a caring family and such
comfortable place to live, because in Guatemala, everyone has so little. I learned that
cannot take anything for granted. I also learned that God could use peoples' passions as
tool to share publicly the reasons why they have put their faith in Jesus Christ.

Jeremiah 1:7-8 (NIV) But The Lord said to me, "Do not say 'I am only a child.' You must g
to everyone I send you to and say whatever I command you to. Do not be afraid of them, fo
I am with you and will rescue you," declares the Lord.

Tell

One December night in youth group, my pastor challenged to take a stand for God and d
something that could help reach out to our friends. I was in 8th grade, and before this night
I had never really been so engaged in a service at youth group. That night something wa
different. I felt God place a dream in my heart - start a Bible study in the middle school.

I went home that night excited to tell my parents about the night. I told my dad, anc
immediately we started thinking of what I should do to start this. About a few weeks later, a
little before Christmas break, I approached my principal and told him what I wanted to dc
and handed him a paper detailing the schedule. He told me he thought it was a fabulous
idea, but he would have to clear it with the superintendent and school board.

The first day I came back from Christmas break, the principal came up to me and said
could start the Bible study. I was so pumped. When the next week rolled around, I started
the bible study. To my amazement, 30 students showed up. It was so cool to be able to tel
my friends what God had done in my life. I had the chance once or twice a month to speak
at the bible study the rest of the year. By the end of the year, the Bible study had grown tc
39 people, and I'm ecstatic to say the group is still successful today.

Looking back on the whole experience, I learned that God's timing is perfect. God put this
dream in my heart at a perfect time, and I was able to share my faith with my friends as a
middle schooler. All of my friends' faith grew along with mine. I am still seeing effects from
this Bible study in some of my friends.

It was amazing to me to see that God could use me, a shy eighth grader, to share my friends
experiences about Jesus Christ in school.

really grew in my faith that year and have continued to use the opportunities God has given me to share my faith with people at my school. I realize now that God gives all of us plenty of opportunities to tell. We just have to take those opportunities to make an impact on others.

What dream has God placed in your heart? From personal experience, I know what it is like to be scared because I was that shy eighth grader. You just need to take that step of faith because God says, "Do not be afraid, for I am with you."

Daily Watermark Challenge

What is a dream God has placed in your heart?

Who can you talk to help you make that dream come true?

What are some steps you can take today to set that dream into motion?

Can you use the everyday opportunities God gives you to share your faith with someone today?

Are you willing to go and do what God calls you to do?

Week in review

Which devotional was most challenging to you this week, and why?

What is one thing God has challenged you to do this week? What's your plan to change

Describe how you have grown in your relationship with the Lord this week.

Chapter 6

Week #4
Devotionals
Stories from Mission Trip Veterans

Challenges for the Week:

Read One Devotional per day. Answer the questions in the Daily Watermark Challenge with more than a one-word answer, put some thought into your responses.

Read: 2 chapters of the Old Testament, 2 chapters of the New Testament, 2 Psalms and a Proverb each day.

Memorize:
Ephesians 2:8 – For it is by grace you have been saved, through faith, and this is not from yourselves, it is the gift of God.
1 Peter 5:7 – Cast all your anxiety on Him because He cares about you.

Prayer. Take 15 minutes or more; pray through the revolving calendar, practice praying conversationally with others.

Develop your story: You have picked a story, now write it out, practice out loud a few times, and ask your pastor if you could share your story at church.

Allen
Trip Location: Montego Bay, Jamaica
Occupation: Anesthesiologist

Highlights: I enjoyed sports and children's ministries with the local youth and getting outside of my comfort zone leading an outreach team. My most memorable moment was watching young kids playing soccer barefoot on a rocky dirt field with a deflated soccer ball, and having the time of their lives.

1 Thessalonians 5:18 (NIV) Give thanks in all circumstances, for this is God's will for you i Christ Jesus.

Live

When you think of Jamaica what comes to mind? Perhaps it is amazing beaches pictured o postcards or a tropical paradise perfect as a honeymoon destination. Some think of stee drum bands and Reggae music. Most do not think of an island that was devastated by hurricane. As a teenager heading out of the country for the first time, I was excited. I preparing for my first missions trip, I had prayed that I would have an impact on the peopl of Jamaica and that I would grow closer to God. As it turns out, I got it backwards. I di grow spiritually, but it was the people of Jamaica that would make the impact on me

As we drove inland on our first day, I saw the results of Hurricane Gilbert. Less than a yea earlier, the entire island had been swarmed over by what was then the most intens hurricane ever in the Atlantic (by comparison Hurricane Katrina ranks #5). It claime hundreds of lives, left over 25% of the entire island homeless, and crippled the economy As I peered out the window of the bus on our drive to the little church in the mountains, w passed many homes that had been "rebuilt". Most were without windows and ha questionable roofs, and I would later learn many were still without indoor plumbing o running water. Over the next ten days, our group participated in many positive program and saw numerous souls come to Christ through outreach. It was incredible to be a part o and yet, for me, there was something else that made all the activities pale in comparison people.

I discovered a people that were still impacted by the devastation of Gilbert yet lived wit passion and sincere gratitude for each need met. I saw a genuine thankfulness for th things that mattered most. Many believers that attended the small church from which w were based had seen their physical security of shelter, health, and finances severel impacted by the hurricane. They still gave thanks. They knew--as did Joseph, Moses, Jol Esther, Paul, and countless others in the Bible--that circumstances and situations shoulc not dictate thankfulness. Rather, they were thankful for the eternal blessings of God. The praised Him for sending his Son and were grateful for the forgiveness of sin. Many of thes families I came into contact with earned less income in a full year than the cost of m mission trip itself, and quite a few still faced challenges meeting their basic needs. Even so they understood gratitude, thankfulness, and not taking blessings for granted far deepe an I did. Here I was, the soon-to-be Bible college student, sent to help bring the Gospel to em, yet I left having learned so much more from them than I could have ever taught. The p sparked in me a spirit of generosity, gratitude, and thankfulness that I pray always ys central to my faith.

ost of us have never truly known need, certainly not need as is seen in other parts of the rld. The Lord has blessed us as Americans with so much we often take for granted; these ings that are luxuries to billions of people. Begin praying that God would open your eyes the needs of others, both at home and on your trip, and that He may create in you a spirit generosity and giving.

Daily Watermark Challenge

hat are you most thankful for in your life? Why?

e there people in your life that deserve thanks from you, but you have yet to express ur gratitude? Make a list and make a point of telling them personally how you feel.

sk yourself/pray that the Holy Spirit would reveal what blessings in life you have taken r granted.

hink about the skills that God has blessed you with that you can be eternally thankful for. egin praying that you will have opportunities to share these eternal blessings with others n your mission trip.

Allysa
Trip Location: Ecuador
Occupation: Low Income Housing Manager

Ministry highlights: Experiencing cultures, the food, miracles, times that God used me to touch the lives of others made my trip to Ecuador memorable.

What I learned from the trip: Since then, I have experienced many miracles (on and off the mission field) through prayer. I know God has a great purpose for me and for you. If you listen, have faith, and believe that God can, you will be amazed by the results.

Jeremiah 29:11 (NIV) For I know the plans I have for you, says the Lord. They are plans for good and not for disaster, to give you a future and a hope.

Live

I remember getting ready for a nighttime rally in Ecuador. Two of my teammates and were going around handing out flyers and praying in the community where we wer working. We would chat with people on the street and occasionally we would walk righ into homes to give out the flyers. One time, I was praying and walking up to a house, and a I was greeting the family, a stray dog came charging at me with its lips curled and teet showing. I had no time to react at all. The dog came up to my leg and started to nudge m leg with its closed mouth. It backed up and growled at me, showing its teeth and an ope mouth. Then repeated hitting my leg with a closed mouth. I could not believe what I wa experiencing. This dog could not open its mouth to bite me, and it was confused. Whe events like this happen, it starts to build your faith in the impossible. When you star believing that God can do the impossible, He will. These experiences will stay with m forever to remind me when I am back at home not to get comfortable with where I am i my relationship with God.

I grew up in a Christian family attending church, going to youth group, and experiencin the summer camp high. I was always told about the importance of prayer, but I guess, took it too lightly. I would pray but not really think that anything would result from m prayers. The faith part was missing. Through my mission experiences, I have seen th importance of prayer and faith and experienced it for myself. Because of these experiences prayer is now a part of my everyday life, and I am constantly in awe of the amazing things i brings about; God actually listens to me and answers.

A Christian life has its ups and downs just like a roller coaster. There are times when yo feel close to God and times you don't. I believe that God has ways to rekindle that fire and awaken your soul with missions being one of those ways. It is a time that you are expectin an experience with God, so therefore, the unexplainable can happen because you expect i What if we could bring that home and expect God to do something in our own back yard What would happen if we brought the faith and prayer life from a foreign land to ou comfort zone?

What is something you have been praying about but struggling in your faith to see it happen?

What fears do you have that are keeping you from getting closer to God?

If you could ask God for one more thing to help you grow in your faith, what would it be and why?

What are the roadblocks in your life that are keeping you from a closer relationship with the Lord?

What is practical one way you are going to live your life by faith, today?

Jacinta
Trip Location: Santiago, Chile
Occupation: Middle School Science Teacher

Ministry highlights: Ministering in schools and churches. Having the opportunity to meet the President of Chile and our choir had the privilege of performing for him as well as pray over him.

Romans 8:28 (NIV) And we know that all things work together for good to them that love God, to them who are the called according to his purpose.

Live

I enjoyed school and looked forward to starting my senior year in high school. I had waited for three long years of high school, and the time had finally come to become the admired looked-up-to senior! The year was off to a great start, and I was excited about all of the fun in store and the great memories to be made. What I didn't know that my year was about to drastically change. It was the second week of school, and I had a terrible accident during soccer game. Playing defense was exciting, but this game brought more than I had hoped for. At just the right time, my leg was sandwiched in between two other players as we all went to kick the soccer ball. I did not win. I ended up with several fractures in my leg. My senior year took a very unexpected turn.

It was a challenging next several weeks as I underwent surgery, adjusted to life for a short time in a wheel chair, hobbled around on crutches and missed out on a lot of school. I was pretty disappointed and had a hard time understanding why my year had been completely changed. It took some time to process and accept my situation. I knew that God was in control, but it was hard to understand why this had happened. My family was very helpful and I developed friendships that I probably wouldn't have otherwise.

At the time of the injury and several weeks and months after, I felt that I was missing out on so much. After some time had passed, I began to realize that the Lord was using my situation for a much bigger plan. He allowed me to build relationships with new friends and family members. He also kept me from making poor choices with other friends. I knew that the Lord had protected me and used my situation to bring glory to Him.

The Lord uses our situation to bring good things, even when we can't see past our situation.

Have you been surprised by something in your life? I experienced a very unexpected turn in my life that brought some difficult situations. Through those challenges, the Lord worked in my heart and showed me that He was in control. He can use challenges to help us grow in Him.

What circumstances in my life are unexpected or not what I thought they would be?

Is there anything in my life that didn't turn out like I expected?

Have I been disappointed by the outcome of something I really looked forward to that turned out very differently? How has God worked in those situations?

What is God trying to teach me when I face unexpected circumstances?

How can God use my life when things don't turn out like I expect?

Jake
Trip Location - Panama City, Panama
Occupation - High School Senior

Ministry highlights - We went to the same school every day and spoke to different groups of people every time. We focused on the abuse at home that some students were experiencing and prayed for them. We also performed skits and shared testimonies to reach out to the kids.

I John 5:14-15 (NIV) And this is the confidence which we have before Him, that, if we ask anything according to His will, He hears us. And if we know that He hears us in whatever we ask, we know that we have the requests that we have asked from Him.

Prayer

At age sixteen, I had the amazing opportunity to go to Panama for ten days. I had never been on my own for more than a day. So, for ten days, being away from my parents and siblings was tough. Nevertheless, I decided to go because it would be fun, and I would be able to hang out with some of my best friends. I was expecting to have a blast but not so much in a spiritual realm of things.

I had gone on a mission trip the previous year to Costa Rica on a basketball trip. The trip was with my dad. It was a memorable trip, but I was missing intimate time with God. I definitely grew in my walk with God, but I didn't have that time where it seemed that everything in life was forgotten for a few moments leaving just God and me. On June 2012, I met God, and it changed my life.

Nine days into the trip, I wasn't focused on prayer time at all. I was focused on having fun. On the last night, our missionary was going to speak to us. We had pizza right before the service, and I just wanted to go back to my room and chill with my buddies. I didn't want to listen to someone for a half hour. So I sat there, and honestly didn't listen to a word he said. I, still to this day, don't remember what he talked about. I do remember, however, what the altar call was. He just said to find a spot in the room and starting seeking out God. So I did, but I was praying halfheartedly. I wasn't trying hard. Suddenly, He said "You guys are going to get out of this what you put into this, really go after God for these last couple minutes." So, I decided to start praying. I asked God to show me His love, show me He cares about me. Instantly, God gave me three areas of focus for my life.

Number one: To start being a leader not a follower.
Number two: To start having my faith be my own, not my parents.
Number three: To start witnessing to my basketball team, because they needed help.

I wondered how this showed God's love. I was thinking; "Cool, those are good ideas" I was not thinking about bringing it home and using those three ideas. Then, unexpectedly, my youth pastor came over and starting praying for me. His exact words, "Dear God, I thank you for Jake. I just pray that you would give him the strength to start being a leader, not a ollower. I also pray that you would help Jake to make his faith become his own, not his arents. Lastly, I pray that you would help him witness to his teammates on his sports eams, especially his basketball team. Thank you God for Jake." I was speechless; God gave ny youth pastor the same exact prayer he gave me, almost word for word. It really put into erspective the importance of prayer and what it can do. That one prayer proved to me ow much God cares about me.

'rayer is really important in our walk with God. Prayer is the pathway that connects you to God. In order for prayer to work, it has to be continuous. You have to want to seek out God. Thessalonians 5:16-18, says "Rejoice always, pray continually, give thanks in all ircumstances; for this is God's will for you in Christ Jesus." Prayer is a rewarding choice. ou get out of it what you put into it.

Daily Watermark Challenge

low has your prayer walk been this far during watermark?

Have you ever had a moment like I did in Panama? And if so, when?

What are three areas in your life needing a prayer focus?

How are you going to change your prayer life today?

Shannon
Trip Locations: L.A. Dream Center and St. Petersburg, Russia
Occupation: Aveda Salon and Spa – co-owner

Ministry highlights: Looking into the eyes of another person who has endured a journey I could never understand... to see the beauty of the being they are, to see Him in them, and then to speak life into this person. Don't let fear, embarrassment, or time get in your way- you might be the only person to ever speak value and love to this person. Be Love to this person. Impact one life. What is life if we cannot stop and love someone?

Psalm 46:10 (NIV) Be still and know that I am God.

Live

This verse came alive to me one day, and I pondered what it meant to literally be still and allow Him to be God. So, I did just that. I sat still and allowed Him to begin to unveil His heart to me, showing me the deep recesses of His heart, and He began guiding my life in a new direction towards intimacy with Him.

Literally practicing Psalm 46:10 is how I began to seek Him. No matter how busy the day is, I create a space to just be still and wait for Him to come. His raw presence invading your life and being completely real with Him is where everything changes. This gives your mission trip a meaning beyond a great group of people getting to travel to another city, state, or nation. Do you know Him this way? Do you want to?

Turn on some soft instrumental music, come empty handed (no Bible, no notebook, no agenda, just you), find a comfortable space where you can be still without falling asleep. This is probably one of the hardest things we can do because we are simply waiting for Him to come. As things are swirling around in your mind, begin to focus on Psalm 46:10, "Be still and know that I am God." Allow His presence to come.

Some people feel a liquid peace, almost subconscious feeling; others feel electricity or goose bumps, some feel a literal presence in their room. You'll know His presence once you've felt it. In His presence we find our identity. We gain His perspective, His heart for the world and each life we encounter. This will impact more than your mission trip. It will impact your everyday life, your daily mission in becoming a genuine person who pursues Christ because we know Him and get to share Him with others.

This is the secret place where His people are empowered to do great exploits. His presence is so great. In one moment of the Lord's presence, He can do what it would have taken us years to do in our own strength. Spending ten minutes alone with Him can alter your day. Grabbing your Bible to take up your Sword of the Spirit equips you to bring His Kingdom to earth. He wants to speak to you personally. Intimately. Directly. This God we want to share with others, do we know Him personally, or are we just going by what our parents have told us, what our pastors have told us? Do you want your mission trip to impact lives beyond your understanding?

t all starts with intimacy. Out of this place flows perfect love. He's waiting for you there. He always is. Allow Him to love you today.

Daily Watermark Challenge

How do you enjoy spending time with the Lord?

Describe how His presence feels to you. If you haven't felt His presence, ask Him to

What is the most important thing you want in your relationship with the Lord?

Take ten minutes in your morning and just sit with the Lord, asking Him what's in His heart for the day. Write down what He shares with you. Keep asking Him questions, leaning into His heart, getting to know Him. It's beautiful!

Sam
Trip Location: Bahamas
Occupation: Youth Pastor

Ministry highlights: This was my first mission trip, so everything was new. I was able to make friends that I'm still connecting with 17 years later. God stretched me to give Him more than I thought I could. He also showed me how He could provide before, during, and after our trip.

Philippians 4:11-13 (CEB) I'm not saying this because I need anything, for I have learned how to be content in any circumstance. I know the experience of being in need and of having more than enough; I have learned the secret to being content in any and every circumstance, whether full or hungry or whether having plenty or being poor. I can endure all these things through the power of the one who gives me strength.

A Time to Serve

In the summer of 1996, I was able to go on my very first mission trip to the Bahamas. I know you're thinking, he really had to suffer for Jesus, right? But this trip had all sorts of lessons God wanted to teach our team. For me, God wanted to show me how life wasn't about having everything perfect or exactly how I thought it should be. One of the first few days after our arrival, I became mad at my leaders because they took the fan from my room. Now this may not seem like a big deal, but I'm telling you, I kind of freaked out. I hate being hot, so when they took it, I felt like the trip was going to be ruined. The leaders graciously gave the fan back after my little tantrum, but God decided to not let it end there. I had a chance to serve my leaders, and I blew it.

Later in the trip, I spent some time with the person who drove our team around the island. His name was Jimmy, and he was one of the most happy, kind, servant-hearted people I had ever met. Jimmy used his own truck to transport us; he spent time with us away from his family and took time off his job just to take care of some students from the United States. After talking to him, I learned when Jimmy was a little boy, he was walking on the beach and bent over to pick something up he noticed in the sand. It happened to be a live grenade, which proceeded to blow off his hand. Here he was all these years later serving our team and us. Did he once complain to us about what happened to him? No! God showed me what it meant to be content, regardless of what happened in life. I missed a chance to serve my leaders, but Jimmy showed me what true service looks like. He inspired me to give my all the rest of the trip and to serve as often as I could, and that's what I strived to do.

As you prepare and go on your trip, you will be faced with challenges. The food might scare you, the team leaders might not lead how you want, or the schedule might not be exactly how you thought it would go. Those things can and will happen, but guess what - It doesn't matter! If you are going to be a servant leader, you are saying to God and yourself, " I don't care what I face; I'm giving my all!" You can serve anyone, anytime, anywhere, the choice is yours.

What is something you're holding on to that doesn't really matter?

Give it to God now in prayer.

What is one way you can serve your church, school, or community today? Write it down and start making things happen!

If Christ can do anything, what dream is He asking you to believe Him for today?

Choose one person you trust to share that dream with and ask them to pray with you about how it can come true.

Week in review

Which devotional was most challenging to you this week, and why?

What is one thing God has challenged you to do this week? What's your plan to change?

Describe how you have grown in your relationship with the Lord this week.

Chapter 7

Week #5
Devotionals
Stories from Mission Trip Veterans

Challenges for the Week:

Read One Devotional per day. Answer the questions in the Daily Watermark Challenge with more than a one-word answer, put some thought into your responses.

Read: 2 chapters of the Old Testament, 2 chapters of the New Testament, 2 Psalms and a Proverb each day.

Memorize:
Hebrews 12:2 - Fixing our eyes on Jesus, the pioneer and perfecter of faith. For the joy set before Him He endured the cross, scorning its shame, and sat down at the right hand of the throne of God.
John 10:10 - The thief comes only to steal and kill and destroy; I have come that they may have life, and have it to the full.

Prayer. Take 15 minutes or more, pray through the revolving calendar, pray for the trip leaders, other team members, Missionary, national church, ministry opportunities.

Develop your story: Daily practice giving your story until you can speak it without notes. Look for opportunities to share your story, speak it with confidence, voice inflection, and emotions.

Rachel
Trip Location: Mexico City, Mexico
Occupation: Bank Loan Officer

Ministry highlights: Working with local churches to serve their neighborhoods by putting outreaches in the streets and having the opportunity to tell my testimony to crowds of people were unforgettable. Climbing to the top of the Teotihuacan Pyramids was amazing.

What I learned from the trip: Most of the time the Lord doesn't want us to be the flashy, huge outreach. He wants to use us to show others His love through our acts of service. That is what changes the hearts of people the most.

Matthew 15:37-40 (ESV) Then the righteous will answer him, saying, Lord, when did we see you hungry and feed you, or thirsty and give you drink? And when did we see you a stranger and welcome you, or naked and clothe you? And when did we see you sick or in prison and visit you? And the King will answer them, Truly I say to you, as you did it to one of the least of these brothers of mine, you did it to me.

Serve—Be the Hands and Feet of Christ

Waking up the morning we were scheduled to fly to Mexico City for our AIM trip, I was so excited to once again head to Mexico! My family and I had gone on several mission trips to Mexico over the past years, so I had high expectations that we would be doing similar tasks on this trip as we did on those previous ones. I was used to putting on spectacular outreaches in poorer neighborhoods, setting up huge distribution sites of clothes, food, and blankets for homeless people, and going to big state prisons to share the Gospel with those in need. I quickly realized that this type of ministry was not in store for us this time.

Our first day in Mexico City welcomed us with thick, hazy smog. We arrived at the first little church we were to assigned to assist. The pastor was grateful for our coming, and immediately began explaining what we were there to do—pick up garbage all around the neighborhood and paint the outside of the church with "homemade paint" (paint-powder and...Coca-Cola). As I brushed the small building with the sticky paint, I remembered questioning the purpose of this mission. Why did we come all this way to pick up some trash and paint a small church?

The next day we went to a different, larger church. I was excited and thought that we must be doing some sort of outreach or distribution! But once again, we were assigned to clean the building for the morning. That afternoon, we did have a small street outreach with that church, but there weren't hundreds of people watching like what I was used to.

At the end of that outreach, there were a handful of people who gave their lives to Christ, and it was then that I realized that this was why we were called there. It didn't matter that we were doing the "grunt" work for these people; we were being the hands and feet of Christ. After feeling ashamed at thinking myself "better" than the work we were given, I humbled myself and let the Lord work through me the rest of the trip. We didn't do any xtravagant prison ministry visits or distributions, but I know that we were there doing vhat Christ wanted us to do—serve those people. It was one of my favorite missions trips I ad the opportunity to experience.

Daily Watermark Challenge

Vhat are some areas in your life where you can ask the Lord to help you become more umble? (school work, sports, obeying your parents, etc...)

Read Matthew 15:37-40 again. Is that relevant to our society and culture today? If so, how?

Think of some ways that you can be a servant where you are now—your school, work, or even your church.

How can you start to prepare your heart to be the hands and feet of Christ for your upcoming mission trip?

Make a list of three people that you feel the Lord is leading you to serve in this season of your life. Now pray about how to bring that plan to action.

Josiah
Trip location: Philippines
Occupation: Youth Pastor

Ministry highlights: I was able to spend the majority of my time talking in front of classrooms and sharing my testimony. I had so many students come up and talk to me after and share how they were going through the same experiences. I also had the pleasure, on two accounts, to enjoy a Filipino delicacy called balut; look it up!

1 Corinthians 9:19-23 (NLT) When I am weak with those who are weak, I share their weakness, for I want to bring the weak to Christ. Yes, I try and find common ground with everyone, doing everything I can to save some.

Live

During the summer between my junior and senior years of high school, I had the opportunity to go to the Philippines. I hadn't ever left the country before; Canada doesn't count. I was a little nervous, but I knew that this was something God was calling me to do. As the trip started, I had several situations that took me far outside of my comfort zone. I was used to eating what I wanted, using a bathroom where I had toilet paper, and showering whenever I needed. All of these luxuries were no longer an option. Slowly, I began to push myself in each one of these areas; this lead to me pushing myself further in other areas of my life while I was on my trip. Even though I knew hardly any of the native language, I began to walk up to people and start conversations. I volunteered to be part of a skit, which terrified me. I ate whatever food was placed in front of me. I began to notice a change in my heart during the trip. This change only happened because I made the choice to change my attitude. One of the girls on the trip was very open about being a vegetarian. At different times on the trip, she refused to eat the food because of the meat that was in it. Even though she wasn't meaning to, she was offending the people taking care of us. We are allowed to have certain freedoms at home, but when God calls us to do something, we need to be willing to go outside of our comfort zone and perhaps even give up some of our freedoms so we can reach the people around us.

As a youth pastor, I minister to all different types of students. I need to be willing to stretch myself and continually go outside of my comfort zone so that I can reach the students where they are at instead of expecting them to come to me. Paul said that he became all things to all people so that some may be saved. We need to have the attitude and the heart that Paul had so God can use us wherever He needs us.

If something in your life seems to be falling down around you, spend time in quiet prayer to figure out what God is trying to teach you through the hardship. Just as a parent uses difficult circumstances to teach his/her children about life, so does the Heavenly Father use life's difficulties to bring us closer to Him.

n what areas are you afraid to step outside of your comfort zone?

How can you practically start to step out in those areas right now so that you will be ready for God to use you on your trip?

What could you accomplish right now in your church and school if you were willing to push yourself outside of your comfort zone?

What opportunities has God placed in your life right now that you can use to push your comfort level?

Is there anything in your attitude that needs to change so that God can use you to your fullest ability?

Phil
Trip Location: Quetzaltenango, Guatemala
Occupation: Missionary to Sweden

Ministry highlights: God impacted my heart to think outside of myself. As an 18 year old who had just started believing in Christ, I was blessed to pray for kids in a TB hospital, see great pastoral leaders making spirit-led decisions, and make a few memories with my fellow teammates!

Hebrews 11:1-2 (NLT) Faith is the confidence that what we hope for will actually happen; it gives us assurance about things we cannot see. Through their faith, the people in days of old earned a good reputation.

Tell

Tim, my colleague, and I visited Kiruna, Sweden - a town found above the Arctic Circle. After a very late night of travel, we started our day by praying to God to lead our steps in faith and started walking around the town.

Perched high on a hill in the center of town of Kiruna is the Swedish Lutheran Church. The decor and architecture suggested Sami and Viking influence to the high-steepled, wood-beamed behemoth.

We walked inside, shook off the winter cold, and continued to pray everywhere our feet fell. Alone in the church, we were joined after 15 minutes by a young woman, marveling at the art and the vast interior of the building. From Tim's encouragement, I approached her speaking Swedish, asking a question. The surprise in her face stopped me, and in her Australian accent, she laughingly told us that she didn't know a bit of the language.

Susan (*name has been changed) had once been a construction project manager in Australia. After intense schooling and eight years of work, she had a midlife crisis. She felt that she hadn't really lived life up to that point and decided to see the world. After five months of her travels, that very morning on the train, she had opened up her window to be greeted by the first snow she had seen in her life! At that moment, she whispered something to herself, "I've been searching for something. I think I'm about to find it."

We had a long conversation about life, God, and searching. Susan shared her perspective about the enormous painted mural of rays of sunlight streaming from heaven to a green pasture below. We spent much of our time listening to her passion for life!

At one point, I shared, "Susan, you've travelled to the far North of Sweden, and who do you meet but two people who also are fluent in English. I believe that this is not coincidence. I do believe in the living God that this church building was built to honor. God has ordered our steps to meet together here. We want to let you know that whatever you have been searching for can be found in Jesus Christ." She had never heard of the message of Jesus Christ before! Jesus was the reason that we met in the first place! Our conversation continued, and we prayed with her for a safe journey and for God to reveal more of who He is to Susan. What an exciting way to say goodbye! This is just one of the many stories from a single trip to Kiruna, where by faith, God surprised us again and again!

We had no earthly idea of what we would encounter that day as Tim and I prayed 'lead our steps, Lord'! Hebrews 11:1-2 encourages us that by the substantial assurance inside of us, we can step into the unknown! As we do this, others will be inspired to follow God as we do according to verse 2. Our steps will quicken the steps of others as reputation inspires faith to do likewise.

Stepping out in the unknown by faith is an idea that is 'nice' to think about, write about, and speak of. It's romantic. Taking the step into the unknown, physically, is another thing altogether. Yet, by faith, we actually are stepping out of the unknown-by-man and into the known-by-God.

As we all strive to make disciples for Christ throughout the world, I dare you to take the step out of the unknown-to-man and into the known-by-God!

You have one life to live, why not spend it on faith that is inspiring, that honors God in faith!

Daily Watermark Challenge

To take a step in faith, it means that you are going to change your spiritual location and inevitably your physical location as well. Are you willing to move out of your comfort zone in order to follow God?

Without tangible evidence, can it be difficult to trust God?

We have access to have assurance from God in what he sees! Do you usually trust your practical circumstances instead of taking a step?

Write about a time where you stepped out in faith.

Pray for God to lead your steps today!

Christina
Trip Location: Guatemala City, Guatemala
Occupation: Department of Defense

Ministry highlights: Visiting and serving at a TB hospital and various schools/orphanages, praying alongside of those hungry for God. Serving alongside my fellow students, while strengthening our faith and trust in God provided unforgettable memories.

2 Peter 1:3-11 (NIV) His divine power has granted to us all things that pertain to life and godliness, through the knowledge of Him who called us to His own glory and excellence, for this very reason, make every effort to supplement your faith with virtue, and virtue with knowledge, and knowledge with self-control, and self-control with steadfastness, and steadfastness with godliness, and godliness with brotherly affection, and brotherly affection with love. For if these qualities are yours and are increasing, they keep you from being ineffective or unfruitful in the knowledge of our Lord Jesus Christ.

Serve – Being Effective and Fruitful

While preparing, I remember feeling overjoyed that God had called me to go on this mission trip. I had always dreamed of doing BIG things for God and this was my opportunity. I spent a lot of time in prayer, reading God's word, raising money, and thinking about how I was going to be used in a BIG way. And because I had been a Christian for nearly half of my life at the time of this AIM trip, I knew I was prepared…or so I thought.

Well, during the first few days of the trip, I completely lost sight of my reason for being there. I had let a series of events cripple my attitude and my willingness to be a servant. I knew I was called to be there and was to be used by God in many ways, but I wasn't able to look past my own selfishness. It did not take too long after this to realize that while I had prepared to be on this trip spiritually and emotionally, I had let the idea of doing something BIG for Christ get in the way of me having the right attitude on the trip.

In retrospect, I believe God used this mission trip to teach me about being an effective and fruitful follower of Christ in the little, day-to-day things. I let go of the idea of doing something BIG for the Lord and focused my attention on who God wants me to be wherever I'm at in life. So, when I'm sorting, washing, and folding an endless pile of my family's laundry, I know it's not about WHAT I'm doing, but WHO God wants me to be while I'm doing these tasks. It's not always the BIG and extravagant outward signs, but it's more about the person God wants you to be in the everyday things you do in life.

Is there anything keeping you from being the person God wants you to be?

In what ways can you become more effective and fruitful?

Are you living for Christ, and are you doing so firmly? Do you know why you live?

What are some practical ways you can supplement your faith with the qualities mentioned in 2 Peter 1:3-11?

Jen
Trip Location: L.A. Dream Center
Occupation: 2nd Grade Teacher

Ministry highlight: Distributing food to families in need, Feeding the homeless, ministering to homeless teens. Cleaning up the neighborhood through "Adopt a Block", and visiting a Mega-church that really knew how to "Have Church", created fond memories for me.

Acts 2:1-2 (NIV) When the day of Pentecost came, they were all together in one place. Suddenly a sound like the blowing of a violent wind came from heaven and filled the whole house where they were sitting.

Pray

I have been a Christian as long as I can remember. I was a little, five-year-old girl at Lake Geneva Bible Camp when I asked Jesus into my heart. Growing up as a child, I went to church at least three times a week and church was always a huge part of who I was. My family was all involved in church, and I knew from the time I was a teenager that I wanted to marry a pastor. Christianity was all I knew, but I also wanted to have experiences that were my own, not experiences that were part of me because of my heritage and upbringing.

Prayer is a daily part of my life. It is really just a conversation between my best friend and myself. I have certain times in my life where prayer has been extremely real to me, but never as real as in April 2002 in Los Angeles, California. We had a little extra time as half of the team was still out ministering. One of the men that we were with asked if we wanted to go to the Bonnie Brea house. The Bonnie Brea house is where the Pentecostal movement started. In 1906, William Seymour held a Bible study at the Bonnie Brea home. This began a revival that lasted until 1915, which included people witnessing intense worship services, speaking in tongues, miracles, and healings.

When entering the Bonnie Brea house, I felt a total presence of God. It was amazing to think that this is where my heritage began. This is where my entire life's purpose was started. This is why I was created. This is where the most important part of my life began - my Christian heritage. Money, friends, my job, none of this would be anything without my rock, Jesus.

Have you ever had that time in your life when you looked back and thought, "When did I feel the closest to God?" This was that pivotal point in my life, standing, holding hands with other believers, in a circle and singing "Holy Ground, I'm Standing on Holy Ground". I had sung that song for years growing up, but never did it seem so real as to be singing it where the Pentecostal movement all started. I envisioned at that time, this is what heaven will be like. We were just a group of ten people that normally would sound like a bunch of off-tune singers, but at that moment, I remember thinking that we sounded better than any group of singers I had ever heard.

There are times in our lives where we need to go back to that moment when we felt God in an overwhelming presence. We all have those times that are filled with questioning God's existence, but it is at those times when we need to remember the important encounters we have had with God. It is at those times when we need to go back and remember why were created. We should live a life that challenges others to find purpose in their lives – to live a life with Christ. It may be sharing Jesus with a friend at school, work, or on a missions trip.

Daily Watermark Challenge

Do you have a place where you experienced God in an overwhelming and real way? Where is that place for you, and why is it monumental in your life?

What are you doing to make sure that you are growing daily in your prayer life? Why is prayer important to you?

How will you someday tell your children about your Christian heritage? Why do you believe what you believe?

How can you make this missions trip one of those unforgettable moments in your life?

Find an older person in your church that you look up to and ask them if they could tell you about a monumental moment in their Christian life?

Kesiah
Trip Location: L. A. Dream Center
Occupation: Stay at Home Mom, working with women with disabilities

Galatians 1:10 (NIV) Am I now trying to win the approval of human beings, or of God? Or am I trying to please people? If I were still trying to please people, I would not be a servant of Christ.

Serve

Have you ever felt intimidated as you approach a new situation? It can be a meeting you may not be looking forward to, or a conversation you need to have with a friend. As you step out in ministry, there will be many things that can easily intimidate you.

I clearly remember a time on my trip that I had the opportunity to minister among some of the numerous homeless people in the Los Angeles area. As I thought about spending time with them, I felt like I needed to have answers to their questions and solutions to all their problems, and if I couldn't completely change their situation, I was a failure.

I thought God had sent me there to change them, but then I realized that wasn't my purpose. God wanted me to treat them with dignity and respect. I believe He wanted me to listen to them and help them accomplish some simple tasks. By doing this, I was validating them as a person rather than someone that society looked down upon.

From Galatians 1:10, the author Paul challenges me to evaluate what my true motives are in every situation: am I trying to win the approval of Man or of God? In which one do I place more value? From whom do I want to receive praise? Looking back to the start of my trip, I hate to admit it, but I was looking for the approval of man. I wanted to solve the problems of the homeless people I was asked to work with, and then was congratulated for doing such an amazing job. My attitude at the start of trip was not where it needed to be. Instead of servanthood, I had an attitude of selfishness.

The trip gave me a new perspective on what God is asking me to do, to serve others. I had many great opportunities to work with people with physical, emotional, and mental needs. I realized that God was not asking me to solve their problems; He was asking me to show love to the people, whom He intensely loves, by serving them.

You don't need to feel intimidated as you look forward to your upcoming trip. You will find yourself in situations where you don't know what to do, and that's ok. It's in those moments that God is giving you the choice: are you seeking the approval of God or of man? Your attitude of servanthood is what God is going to use. It is greater than your talents.

Being honest with yourself today, whom are you trying to win approval of: man or God?

How do you seek to win approval of man? How do you seek to win approval of God?

Looking forward to the trip, what intimidates you the most?

On the trip, what would you like God to change in your life?

What is one thing you can do today to help practice a servant's heart?

Week in review

Which devotional was most challenging to you this week, and why?

What is one thing God has challenged you to do this week? What's your plan to change?

Describe how you have grown in your relationship with the Lord this week.

Chapter 8

A Carry-on full of useful stuff

Influential Adult, Mentor, Coach (Jedi)

Every student that rises to the top of their particular field, whether it be in sports, acting, playing an instrument or creative writing, always has someone to thank for their growth in their skills - a coach. In this 15-week "Watermark" journey, you NEED a coach to speak into your life. So, pick an adult in your church or community that you respect as a strong, mature Christian (preferably not your pastor or someone related to you), and ask them if they would be willing to invest in your life as you prepare for your upcoming trip.

Ask your coach to:
- **Meet with you monthly /weekly - phone, email or text contact is required**
- **Pray the completed revolving prayer calendar with you**
- **Help develop your story – practice it, revise it, give practical advise, etc.**
- **Help keep you accountable for required work – the time in prayer, the word, scripture memorization**
- **Help develop blitz week plan – participate with you**

I agree to invest in: _____over the next three months. I agree to meet with him/her monthly and contact him/her weekly to help keep him/her accountable to the habits that will help him/her grow in their relationship with Jesus Christ. I will pray the revolving prayer calendar with him/her, and help develop his/her story of what God has done in their life - as they prepare to be used by God on this high watermark moment of his/her life.

Signed: _____ Date: _____

Coach (Jedi) – please initial when complete

____ Met with student – month #1   (weekly contacts too)
____ Met with student – month #2   (weekly contacts too)
____ Met with student – month #3   (weekly contacts too)
____ Met with student – month #4   (weekly contacts too)

____ Revolving prayer calendar complete – pray through the calendar with student

____ Helped develop student story

____ Kept student accountable for time in prayer, the word, memory verses – month #1
____ Kept student accountable for time in prayer, the word, memory verses – month #2
____ Kept student accountable for time in prayer, the word, memory verses – month #3
____ Kept student accountable for time in prayer, the word, memory verses – month #4

____ Developed a plan and participated in Blitz week with student

My student completed all the required tasks! Signed: _____

Revolving Prayer Calendar
For each day, Pray for Someone or Something in: my Life, my School, and my Trip

1 - Life _____
    School _____
      Trip _____

2 - Life _____
    School _____
      Trip _____

3 - Life _____
    School _____
      Trip _____

4 - Life _____
    School _____
      Trip _____

5 - Life _____
    School _____
      Trip _____

6 - Life _____
    School _____
      Trip _____

7 - Life _____
    School _____
      Trip _____

8 - Life _____
    School _____
      Trip _____

9 - Life _____
    School _____
      Trip _____

10 - Life _____
    School _____
      Trip _____

11 - Life _____
    School _____
      Trip _____

12 - Life _____
    School _____
      Trip _____

13 - Life _____
    School _____
      Trip _____

14 - Life _____
    School _____
      Trip _____

15 - Life _____
    School _____
      Trip _____

16 - Life _____
    School _____
      Trip _____

17 - Life _____
    School _____
      Trip _____

18 - Life _____
    School _____
      Trip _____

19 - Life _____
    School _____
      Trip _____

20 - Life _____
    School _____
      Trip _____

21 - Life _____
    School _____
      Trip _____

22 - Life _____
    School _____
      Trip _____

23 - Life _____
    School _____
      Trip _____

24 - Life _____
    School _____
      Trip _____

25 - Life _____
    School _____
      Trip _____

26 - Life _____
    School _____
      Trip _____

27 - Life _____
    School _____
      Trip _____

28 - Life _____
    School _____
      Trip _____

29 - Life _____
    School _____
      Trip _____

30 - Life _____
    School _____
      Trip _____

12-Week New Testament Reading Plan

<u>Week #1</u>
Matthew 1 – 3
Matthew 4 – 6
Matthew 7 – 9
Matthew 10 – 13
Matthew 14 – 16
Matthew 17 – 19
Matthew 20 – 23

<u>Week #2</u>
Matthew 22 – 24
Matthew 25 – 28
Mark 1 – 3
Mark 4 – 6
Mark 7 – 9
Mark 10 – 12
Mark 13 – 16

<u>Week #3</u>
Luke 1 – 3
Luke 4 – 6
Luke 7 -9
Luke 10 – 12
Luke 13 – 15
Luke 16 – 18
Luke 19 – 21

<u>Week #4</u>
Luke 22 – 24
John 1 – 3
John 4 – 6
John 7 – 9
John 10 – 12
John 13 – 15
John 16 – 18

<u>Week #5</u>
John 19 – 21
Acts 1 - 3
Acts 4 - 6
Acts 7 - 9
Acts 10 – 12
Acts 13 – 15
Acts 16 – 18

<u>Week #6</u>
Acts 19 – 21
Acts 22 – 24
Acts 25 – 28
Romans 1 – 3
Romans 4 – 6
Romans 7 – 9
Romans 10 – 12

<u>Week #7</u>
Romans 13 – 16
I Corinthians 1 – 3
I Corinthians 4 – 6
I Corinthians 7 – 9
I Corinthians 10 – 12
I Corinthians 13 – 16
II Corinthians 1 – 3

<u>Week #8</u>
II Corinthians 4 – 6
II Corinthians 7 – 9
II Corinthians 10 – 13
Galatians 1 – 3
Galatians 4 – 6
Ephesians 1 – 3
Ephesians 4 – 6

<u>Week #9</u>
Philippians 1 - 4
Colossians 1 - 4
I Thessalonians 1 - 3
I Thessalonians 4 - 5
II Thessalonians 1 - 3
I Timothy 1 - 3
I Timothy 4 - 6

<u>Week #10</u>
II Timothy 1 - 4
Titus 1 - 3
Philemon, Heb. 1 - 2
Hebrews 3 - 5
Hebrews 6 - 8
Hebrews 9 - 11
Hebrews 12 - 13

<u>Week #11</u>
James 1 -3
James 4 - 5, I Peter 1
I Peter 2 - 5
II Peter 1 - 3
I John 1 - 3
I John 4 -5, II John
III John, Jude

<u>Week #12</u>
Revelation 1 - 3
Revelation 4 - 6
Revelation 7 - 9
Revelation 10 - 12
Revelation 13 - 15
Revelation 16 - 18
Revelation 19 - 22

Scriptures to Memorize

Jeremiah 29:11
For I know the plans I have for you, declares the Lord; plans to prosper you and not to harm you, plans to give you hope and a future.

Isaiah 53:5
But He was pierced for our transgressions, He was crushed for our iniquities; the punishment that brought us peace was on Him, and by His wounds we are healed.

Philippians 4:6-8
Do not be anxious about anything, but in every situation, by prayer and petition, with thanksgiving, present your requests to God. And the peace of God, which transcends all understanding, will guard your hearts and your minds in Christ Jesus. Finally, brothers and sisters, whatever is true, whatever is noble, whatever is right, whatever is pure, whatever is lovely, whatever is admirable - if anything is excellent or praiseworthy—think about such things.

John 3:16
For God so loved the world that He gave His one and only Son that whoever believes in Him will be saved.

Matthew 28:19-20
Therefore go and make disciples of all nations, baptizing them in the name of the Father and of the Son and of the Holy Spirit, and teaching them to obey everything I have commanded you. And surely I am with you always, to the very end of the age.

Proverbs 3:5–6
Trust in the Lord with all your heart and lean not on your own understanding; in all your ways submit to him, and He will make your paths straight.

Ephesians 2:8 – For it is by grace you have been saved, through faith, and this is not from yourselves, it is the gift of God.

I Peter 5:7 – Cast all your anxiety on Him because He cares about you.

Hebrews 12:2 - Fixing our eyes on Jesus, the pioneer and perfecter of faith. For the joy set before Him He endured the cross, scorning its shame, and sat down at the right hand of the throne of God.

John 10:10 - The thief comes only to steal and kill and destroy; I have come that they may have life, and have it to the full.

Sample fundraising letter

(Do not copy this word for word. Instead, use it as a guide to write a personal letter)

Dear _____ ,

This summer I have the amazing opportunity of serving on a short-term mission trip to _____. As a part of the team, I will be involved in _____ and _____. I am excited that the Lord has enabled me to be a part of this experience, and I am really looking forward to sharing God's love in _____.

I know that this kind of work is in vain without prayer, so I am asking that you consider praying for me, for our team, and especially for the people I will serve in _____. I also ask that you prayerfully consider contributing financially.

The total amount I need to raise in order to go on the trip is $_____. My deadline to have the necessary funds together is _____. I have faith that God will make it possible.

Please pray with me that this need will be met. I'm excited, hopeful, and expectant that I will learn so much through this experience. I greatly appreciate you letting me share with you what I believe will be one of the most meaningful experiences of my life.

Sincerely,

Add any special donation instructions from your church in this space.
Cut and enclose with donation

I wish to support _____ in their ministry to _____.

Name
Address

One time gift of $_____

___ I cannot support financially but will pray for the team faithfully.
___ I am not able to be involved.

Please make checks payable and mail to:

Sample fundraising letter - 2

(Do not copy this word for word. Instead, use it as a guide to write a personal letter)

Dear _____ ,

I am so excited about this coming summer! A few months ago, I received a brochure about _____, a short-term youth mission opportunity. Every year they send teams of young people into various parts of the world to work together with missionaries and national churches in evangelism.

This year I have been accepted to go to _____ from _____ to _____. As part of the team, I will be involved in _____.
I am really looking forward to this opportunity, but I do need help in raising the necessary money.

The total cost will be _____. While I'm writing because we are friends, I don't want to impose upon our friendship. If you can help in any way, it would be appreciated. Thanks for understanding.

I have three payment deadlines I must meet. The first is _____, the second is _____ , and the final payment must be in by _____.

If you are able to financially support me, please send your *tax deductible* donation prior to these dates. Checks should be made payable to:

(Your Church Name)

(Your church address).

I realize this is a lot of money to raise in a short time, but I have faith it will come. Thanks so much for considering my request and for whatever you can contribute. I really do appreciate you very much. Please keep our trip in your prayers.

Love,

(Your name)

(helpful tip – add some pictures of the country, a flag or a picture of you)

Trip Expectation Letter

Weeks before the trip, prayerfully answer these questions. After you have completed them, seal this sheet in an envelope and open it on the last day of your mission trip or shortly after you return home. I predict you will be amazed at how God has specifically answered these prayers/expectations. Ephesians 3:20 (NLT) "Now all glory to God, who is able through His mighty power at work within us, to accomplish infinitely more than we might ask or think.

How would you like to see God use your team? Describe your dreams.

What would you like to see God do in your life?

How do you desire to be used by God on this trip?

Describe how you would want to be different when this trip is done?

What areas of your life do you need God to change?

What is a specific prayer you need God to answer in your life?

Signed: _____ Date: _____

Tips for Team Members by Jon Dahlager
(Missionary to Costa Rica)

1. **You are here to serve.**
   a. This trip is not about you but serving the Lord and being a blessing to others.
   b. Even more, you are an excuse for the local church to be more effective through the guidance of the missionary.
   c. You will be blessed as you serve.
   d. Codes of expected conduct and appearance are different because of local culture, church rules, and the fact that they consider you "missionaries."
   e. Respect the dress code. Modesty is always important.
2. **You**
   a. Be smart. Don't bring your precious iPhone / iPad, wallet, or purse.
   b. You will be bending your way of life to fit the context of the culture you will be apart of...not vice versa.
   c. Please, Thank You, Respect!
   d. Volume of your mouth. You are a dynamic person; focus on silence.
3. **Time is a commodity**
   a. Spend it wisely. Don't waste it. You are paying for time in another culture in order to affect others toward Christ.
4. **Collect new experiences**
   a. Be a learner, an adventurer. Be curious. Ask questions.
   b. Try lots of new things (food and fun; speaking, acting and being outgoing)
5. **Make new friends**
   a. With team members, national team members, kids in schools and churches.
   b. Your sincere interest, love, and time give human value. They are important!
   c. Don't exaggerate; be honest about your culture.
6. **Examine your life through new lenses**
   a. Imagine yourself in the shoes of your new friends.
   b. What are your excuses or complaints.
   c. What is God speaking to you about your life?
7. **Write it down / blog**
   a. Keep a reflection journal or blog to write down your notes <u>during</u> the trip, not just at the end.
   b. If you wait too long, you will not remember what you were thinking and feeling at the time.
8. **Be careful with personal information**
   a. You can make Facebook friends with the people you spend time with on the trip if you are careful with what you have on facebook.
   b. Take personal information off facebook (address, cell #, etc...)
   c. Do not share your home address!
   d. Do not write love letters.

Helpful Travel Information

Luggage
The maximum size for a carry-on bag for most airlines is 45 linear inches - the total of the height, plus the width, plus the depth of the bag.

The maximum weight for most checked luggage is 50 pounds. Check with the airline you are flying to find out their weight limits. Also, check with your airline to find out the cost of checking luggage for flights. Almost all U.S. domestic flights charge for baggage. Pack all liquids in plastic zip bags.

Immigration/Custom Forms
These can be very intimidating, but don't panic! Here are a few very helpful tips:
- Family name = Last name
- Surname = Last name
- Keep your airline seat assignment card. It contains the date, airline and flight #
- Passport number – for USA passports, nine-digit number at the top of the passport
- Your passport must be signed in pen; without this permanent signature, it is not legal
- For most countries, you need at least six months until the expiration date on your passport (Also, bring along two colored copies, one for your leader, plus one for you to carry)
- Know where you will be staying in the destination country, i.e. church name or motel name, city location, what state/district of the country
- Purpose of the trip question on the security forms: you are a tourist while ministering on your mission trip. This is not a business trip
- Occupation: even if you have a job, but are still a student, write student
- Nationality: United States of America or North American (if you are a U.S. Citizen)
- Most countries require you to use this format for your birth date: Day, Month, Year, i.e. if you were born on June 15, 1998, you would write it: 15–06-1998

Packing List
- Jeans/pants (plan on wearing them more than once)
- T-shirts, tops. (Nothing even perceived to be offensive)
- Dress clothes for church services or ministry
- Modest Shorts (if appropriate for the country/ministry)
- Sweatshirt, coat, or raincoat
- Swimsuit (if swimming is a possibility, please be very modest! Remember whom you are representing)
- Athletic shoes
- Comfortable walking shoes - sandals are cute but might not be the safest
- Enough clothes for the trip - assume no laundry facilities are available
- Work clothes, gloves (if needed)
- Quality pillow, in my opinion, it's worth the size and weight to help you sleep
- Sunglasses
- Towel(s) (Can you use the same towel for 13 days?)
- Cheap flip-flops or sandals to wear in the shower. Be safe!
- Personal hygiene items
- Toiletries (pack them in plastic zip bags to avoid spills)
- Water bottle

- ➢ Plastic bags (they come in handy for dirty clothes)
- ➢ Freezer size plastic zip bags and dryer sheets for stinky shoes, sandals overnight
- ➢ Bible, Journal, Pens
- ➢ Earplugs (you will be thankful if your roommate snores)
- ➢ Small flashlight
- ➢ If you are "that guy", electrical or duct tape, foldable tools (no knives please), sharpie marker, pliers, survival band, zip ties so you can MacGyver anything
- ➢ Inexpensive watch/alarm clock
- ➢ Mini locks (not that they will prevent theft, but it's a deterrent)
- ➢ Pocket-sized translation dictionary
- ➢ Prescription medication (must have your name on the bottle that matches your ID)
- ➢ DO NOT bring any medications you purchased out of the county, unless it is clearly labeled You must also have documentation verifying that a doctor prescribed it
- ➢ Personal medical kit includes:
  - ○ 5 Band-Aids
  - ○ Anti-bacterial cream or wipes
  - ○ Sanitizing wipes or hand sanitizer
  - ○ Over-the-counter medicines: a few Tylenol, Aspirin, ibuprofen, etc.
  - ○ Pepto Bismol (pink bismuth tablets) or Imodium AD for upset stomach
  - ○ Chapstick
  - ○ Sunscreen
  - ○ Bug repellent

Spending Money

You can purchase a lot of souvenirs for a few dollars in most parts of the world. I would suggest between $75-$100. Don't bring Traveler's checks; they are becoming very difficult to cash. Most countries have ATMs at the airport, so you can use your credit card or bankcard to withdraw cash and receive the latest exchange rates. However, you will be charged a healthy foreign currency transfer fee, plus additional fees your bank may attach. Exchange money only with an approved vendor that the missionary or local host points you to. DO NOT exchange your money on the street unless you are a skilled traveler with lots of experience in currency exchange.

Chapter 9

15-Week Discipleship Program

Watermark 2.0

This is an additional program you can work through as you prepare for the upcoming trip. For each of the 15 weeks, a different one of the five habits of a campus leader is explained and highlighted. Simple ideas are given of how to include Prayer, Living, Telling, Serving and Giving into your daily life. You will be challenged to:

Memorize one scripture per week,

A weekly Challenge, practical ways to grow in your faith,

Scripture reading: Two to Three chapters per day (You will read the entire New Testament over the next 15 weeks)

Prayer: Ten to Fifteen minutes per day.

Week #1 – Prayer

Prayer is "a conversation between two people who love each other" (Rosalind Rinker). As you look forward to the trip, prayer is going to be a key part of preparing yourself for what God wants to do in, and through, your life. Oftentimes prayer does more for the person praying than the individual for whom the prayer is lifted; prayer corrects shortcomings in our personal live so God can use you in efforts to help those around you.

Goal: Spend at least ten minutes a day in prayer.

To help keep you focused, completely fill out the **Revolving Prayer Calendar** on the next page. For each day, write in someone or something you can pray for on each of the three lines: my **Life,** my **School**, my **Trip.**

My Life - Pray for friends, family members, struggles or dreams you may have, your future.
My School - Pray for friends, enemies, teachers - good or bad, principals, etc.
My Trip - Pray for missionary or church/pastor you are teaming with, leaders.

Five Friend Focus

Pray for five friends – Pray that God would give you an opportunity to share your story of what Jesus has done in your life. Pray for a blessing over their lives. Pray for the activities they are in, their family, and their future plans. Pray that they would come to see a need for a personal relationship with Jesus Christ

Friend #1 _____

Friend #2 _____

Friend #3 _____

Friend #4 _____

Friend #5 _____

Ask your coach to pray for these five friends and their parents with you.

Memorize: Jeremiah 29:11 - For I know the plans I have for you, declares the Lord; plans to prosper you and not to harm you, plans to give you hope and a future.

Weekly Challenge: Five Friend Focus. Fill out the Revolving Prayer Calendar. Give a copy to your coach for him / her to pray through the list with you.

Scripture Reading: Matthew 1 – 16

Prayer: Take time daily to pray the revolving prayer calendar – Pray for one thing from your life, your school and your upcoming trip.

Week #2 – Live

"Actions speak louder than words" is an old saying that holds considerable truth. Anyone can talk about it, but backing it up with actions is where it becomes real. Are you living a life that is more than just talk? Are you living out your faith at school, at home, on your team, or in your group of friends?

No two people are alike; God has uniquely designed each one for His purpose. To figure out what you are gifted in can open your eyes to what God has for you to accomplish in your life. It does help to know who you are in Christ, so take some time to complete this spiritual gifts inventory. There are many different spiritual gifts listed in scripture; nine are found in I Corinthians 12, and seven are listed in Romans 12. This inventory will help you discover what your gifts may be. It will take about 30 minutes to complete. When you are done, share the results with your coach and your youth pastor/youth leader.

www.buildingchurch.net/g2s-d.htm

Required reading: *How Good Is Good Enough*, by Andy Stanley

Have you ever been asked that question by a friend - "how good do I have to be to make it to heaven?" If you have ever struggled to give a confident answer, or maybe you aren't even sure yourself - this easy book is for you! When you are done, write a one-page report for your coach to read, and then talk about this "eternal" question together.

Optional reading:
Not a Fan by Kyle Idleman
Primal by Mark Batterson
Live To Make A Difference by Max Lucado
The Case for Christ by Lee Strobel
Crazy Love by Francis Chan
Static Jedi by Eric Samuel Timm

Memorize: Isaiah 53:5 - But He was pierced for our transgressions, He was crushed for our iniquities; the punishment that brought us peace was on Him, and by His wounds we are healed.

Weekly Challenge: Pick up one of the books listed above and read it. Then, discuss it with your coach. Complete the spiritual gift inventory and discuss the results with your coach and/or youth pastor.

Scripture Reading: Matthew 17 – Mark 4

Prayer: Take time daily to pray the revolving prayer calendar – Pray for one thing from your life, your school and your upcoming trip.

Week #3 – Give

Matthew 6:21 says "For where your treasure is, there your heart will be also." As a youth pastor, I realized over many years of ministry how true this is. The students that were willing to give money to missions projects rarely faltered in their pursuit of God. This was not always the case, but for the most part, those who were willing to give something they had worked so hard at getting (money and other treasures earned by work) often had a heart of giving. Their heart followed their treasure.

Mission Giving Goal

I challenge you to set a missions goal over the next 11 weeks. Investing in the kingdom of God is a habit that will pay eternal dividends. Look at the cost of your mission trip, take a percentage of the trip, and commit to giving that before the trip begins - a sort of seed offering. If your trip cost $1500, 2% of your trip would be $30. If it cost $199, 15% would be $29.85, etc. Look at the cost of your trip. Then take some time to pray about what God would want you to give before the trip begins. It's NOT a fundraiser, but rather giving out of the money you have earned, that shows where your treasure is! Talk with your youth pastor or youth leader about what projects your group has committed to for the year.

Another idea is to contact the missionary or the ministry you are planning on teaming with for your trip and ask what needs they may have. It could be supplies, electronics, or money to purchase supplies in your mission locale. Try and bless the missionary too. Ask questions like: what is your favorite candy? What food do you miss most from home? If they have children, try and find out what toys, games, food, candy or other fun stuff they may love and miss from home and surprise them with these gifts. Another fun idea for kids; to plan a surprise birthday party for them. Let your team bless them!

Memorize: Philippians 4:6-8 - Do not be anxious about anything, but in every situation, by prayer and petition, with thanksgiving, present your requests to God. And the peace of God, which transcends all understanding, will guard your hearts and your minds in Christ Jesus. Finally, brothers and sisters, whatever is true, whatever is noble, whatever is right, whatever is pure, whatever is lovely, whatever is admirable - if anything is excellent or praiseworthy—think about such things.

Weekly Challenge: Set an 11-week missions goal; communicate your goal to your coach and youth pastor/leader

Scripture Reading: Mark 5 – Luke 4

Prayer: Take time daily to pray the revolving prayer calendar – Pray for one thing from your life, your school and your upcoming trip.

Week #4 – Serve

The trip you are registered for will be fun, every trip is great and most of them have some sort of entertainment elements built into the agenda, but that isn't the reason why this trip has been scheduled. This trip is <u>not about you!</u> It's about serving others so that you can share the love of Jesus with those you come in contact with.   St. Francis of Assisi said, "Preach the gospel always, use words if necessary."

To get into practice of serving others, this week's challenge is for you to volunteer at your church or youth group. Every church has many opportunities for people to serve. Ask your youth pastor/leader or pastor, "How could I serve the church for a couple of hours this week". They will give you some jobs to complete or ministries to help. You must serve with a great attitude, no matter what it is. It will be great practice for the trip; remember, it's NOT about you!

Some simple ideas:
- Volunteer at your church to help out in the nursery or children's programs.
- Join the team that produces the service with technical skills like: sound production, lights, and video.
- Help with traffic in the parking lot.
- Become a greeter at the door and welcome people with a smile to church
- Offer to help with cleaning around the church or yard work
- Put your tech skills to work by volunteering to help teach the older people in the church to use their phones, computers or other electronics they may not fully understand.; most likely you know about technology than 90% of the crowd.

Memorize: Matthew 28:19-20 - Therefore go and make disciples of all nations, baptizing them in the name of the Father and of the Son and of the Holy Spirit, and teaching them to obey everything I have commanded you. And surely I am with you always, to the very end of the age."

Weekly Challenge: Volunteer at least two additional hours at your church or youth group with a great serving attitude!

Scripture Reading: Luke 5 – 21

Prayer: Take time daily to pray the revolving prayer calendar – Pray for one thing from your life, your school and your upcoming trip.

Week #5 – Tell

You took a step of faith and registered for a mission trip, and you have also been recommended by your pastor, meaning you must be living a productive Christian life evident to those around you. You have a story to tell, and on this trip you will have an opportunity to share your story of what God has done in your life. You may be thinking, "What on earth am I going to say?" If you are a follower of Christ, you have a story of forgiveness to tell and stories of when God has answered prayer. If you have confessed your faith in Christ, He has become more than just a story you have read; He has become real to you.

What Makes a Good Story?

- Use a story from your life - You will be an expert at telling it as it's about you!
- Describe something good or bad that happened to you or your family.
- Try to re-tell the story with energy, include emotions you had and feelings you struggled with.
- Give just enough detail in your story to set the stage.
- Take about 2 to 3 minutes (twice as long if it is interpreted).
- Conclude the story with how God appeared, share what He did: How He answered prayer, provided guidance, wisdom, etc.
- Try and answer this question: what one point do I want my listener to remember?
- When sharing your story, try to build rapport with the audience, sharing something they can relate to.
- Use words in your story that a "non-church" person can understand.

What Not to Say

- Don't get political - don't be a proud American
- Don't share information that is too personal
- Don't bore the audience with too much information about stuff they won't understand
- Don't us idioms, like, I had a brain fart, or I totally spaced out, etc.
- Don't use churchy words - redeemed, washed in the blood, I was worshipping, etc.
- Don't include any inside jokes

Your story can bring life! Practice telling it!

Memorize: John 3:16: For God so loved the world that He gave His one and only Son that whoever believes in Him will be saved.

Weekly Challenge: Pick a story from your life, write it out, reread it at least five times, and keep making changes. Work on it with your coach

Scripture Reading: Luke 22 – John 12

Prayer: Take time daily to pray the revolving prayer calendar – Pray for one thing from your life, your school and your upcoming trip.

Week #6 – Prayer

Conversational Prayer - *Pray as if you are talking with a friend*
Drop the idea of trying to impress others with your prayers. Pray honestly from your heart

Praying with Others

- People get bored with long wordy prayers, So, make them short (2-4 sentences long).
- Follow the leading of the Holy Spirit. If He leads you to pray for something, do so - even if it takes you off the current prayer topic. Some people call this popcorn prayer.
- The Holy Spirit is most likely leading someone else to pray for the same thing. They will follow your lead!
- If there is a pause, the leader can move onto the next written prayer request. Before you start, brainstorm things to pray for such as: the trip, the missionary, pastor, team leaders, other team members or schools, principals, teachers and friends.

The Power of Agreement

Matthew 18:19-20 – "Again I tell you that if two of you on earth agree about anything you ask for, it will be done for you by my Father in heaven. For where two or three come together in my name, there I am with them."
I know God acts in response to our prayer, even more when we agree in Jesus' name!

Agree with others during prayer (using non-verbal's, feel free to saying "amen" (so be it!), nodding your head, staying connected during prayer, praying silently - being in agreement with the one praying helps you stay focused too). Being in agreement – brings the power that Matt. 18 references. God hears and answers those types of prayer

Here is an example of what it may sound like:
- brainstorm things to pray for, write them down. The leader starts out in prayer for the trip and the missionary you are working with
- one may echo that prayer for their missionary; three might do the same (others agree)
- as you feel the Holy Spirit leading you, step out and pray for safety on the trip
- someone else may then pray for details like plane connections, favor with the nationals

"Prayer is a conversation between two people who love each other"

Memorize: Joshua 1:9 - Have I not commanded you? Be strong and courageous. Do not be afraid; do not be discouraged, for the Lord your God will be with you wherever you go.

Weekly Challenge: Get together with friends or others from the trip, and practice praying conversationally; pray honestly and from the heart.

Scripture Reading: John 13 – Acts 8

Prayer: Take time daily to pray the revolving prayer calendar – Pray for one thing from your life, your school and your upcoming trip.

Week #7 – Live

Random Acts of Kindness are acts with no desire to be discovered or receive credit for completing. Giving to others without any expectation of getting anything in return. Do them at school, at home, in church, in the community. <u>Do as many things as you can by being anonymous</u>. It is a wonderful feeling. Winston Churchill said, "We make a living by what we get, we make a life by what we give." Here are some practical ideas:

- Thank as many people as you can for things they do for you: store clerk, bus driver, and janitor.
- Open the door for another person.
- Clean up a piece of garbage in school hallway or on the sidewalk.
- Say something nice to everyone you meet today.
- Leave a kind note for a family member or friend.
- Be willing to listen.
- Smile and say "Hello" to people you don't know.
- Offer to babysit for free. Perhaps you know a couple or a single parent that could use your help.
- Offer your place in the grocery check-out line to someone behind you.
- Slap someone on the back and tell him or her thanks.
- Try and make someone laugh today.
- Call a parent just to say you love them.
- Return a shopping cart to the cart corral.
- Check in on someone you know is alone.
- Stop by a nursing home just to spend a little time with the residents.
- Collect canned goods for a local food bank.
- Shovel snow for a neighbor or rake a neighbors lawn.
- Ask someone to pull your finger - it always brings a smile.
- Donate $1 every time you are asked to make a donation to a worthwhile charity.
- Send flowers to a teacher who has dedicated their life to educating children.
- Send someone a hand written note of thanks.
- Give a compliment about your waiter / waitress to his / her manager. (not hitting on her!)
- Send someone a small gift anonymously.
- Give a huge tip to someone when they least expect it.
- Give up your seat for someone - not just an elderly person.
- Write notes of appreciation at least once a week, it's a great habit to begin!
- Give another driver your parking spot.
- Send a thank you note to a person who has helped you in the past.
- Laugh often. A day without laughter is a wasted day , as noted by Charlie Chaplin

Memorize: Proverbs 3:5 – 6: Trust in the Lord with all your heart and lean not on your own understanding; in all your ways submit to him, and he will make your paths straight.

Weekly Challenge: Try committing at least two Random Acts of Kindness per day this week, Try making it a habit! Keep track of them.

Scripture Reading: Acts 9 – 24

Prayer: Take time daily to pray the revolving prayer calendar – Pray for one thing from your life, your school and your upcoming trip.

Week #8 – Give

Sacrifice is a concept very few people understand. It's easy to give but to sacrifice is a tough step of faith! To sacrifice means to step beyond giving, to where it really hurts to give that much. It can be a dollar amount, an amount of time, or a valued possession.

Challenge:

Pray about what you should give away (not money). Ask God: What is one possession I could give away that truly is a sacrifice, that could really bless someone or that could make someone's life easier? Here are some things you could give that would help others in need:

Blood. According to the American Red Cross, currently, only 3 out of 100 people in America donate blood, despite the fact that in America alone, every 2 seconds somebody needs blood. **www.givelife.org.**

Time: With an aging population in America, nursing homes and senior adult care centers would use visitors who would interact with residents. **www.volunteermatch.org.**

Like skills: Consider becoming a mentor for Big Brothers Big Sisters and pass along some of your lessons learned in life. **www.bbbs.org**

Hope: If you are over 18 and in good health, become a possible bone marrow donor. Samples are drawn and put into a nationwide database. **www.bethematch.org.**

Excess stuff: "One man's trash is another man's treasure." The Salvation Army and Goodwill accept quality used items. **www.salvationarmyusa.org**, **www.goodwill.org.**

Life: Be an organ and tissue donor when you renew your driver's license in the event of an unforeseen tragedy. One donor can save as many as 50 lives! **www.organdonor.gov.**

Knowledge: Sometimes, simply being able to share what you know can change someone's life. Become a volunteer tutor, mentor at-risk children, or be a friend to victims of crime, cancer survivors, or bereaved families. Make an impact on someone's life.

Money: Research charities or ministries that help people with needs in areas that interest you. **www.feedone.org**, **www.lacc4hope.org**, **www.worldvision.org**,

Memorize: Ephesians 2:8 – For it is by grace you have been saved, through faith, and this is not from yourselves, it is the gift of God.

Weekly Challenge: Prayerfully decide what to give. Your sacrifice will bless others. Talk with your coach about your decision, and ask them to keep you accountable to complete it.

Daily Reading: Acts 25 – Romans 14

Prayer: Take time daily to pray the revolving prayer calendar – Pray for one thing from your life, your school and your upcoming trip.

Week #9 – Serve

Serving is about the giving of your time and talent to make life easier for someone else. It is about putting your desires and needs behind the cause or person with whom you are engaged. Serving is about investing in something or someone with no strings attached. It is when you, as an individual, activate your willingness. This trip is <u>not about you!</u> So let's put this into practice by serving your current mission field - your school.

> - Pray for your principals, teachers, and coaches.
> - Do your homework, and don't ever cheat!
> - Compliment people for doing good, and don't spread rumors or gossip.
> - Pray daily for the people you like least. Pray for each person in your class by name.
> - Befriend a janitor. Be nice to the lunch lady; she will treat you right.
> - Look people in the eye when they are talking.
> - Keep a great attitude, even when things go wrong.
> - Make people laugh; be fun to be around.
> - Treat everyone with respect, take people seriously, and avoid hurtful words.
> - State your opinions with grace and respect; avoid being negative or critical.
> - Give your best effort in the classroom; give your best effort to your team.
> - Live with an authentic faith; don't just talk about it.
> - Invite a friend to your youth group.
> - Go to your friends' events and cheer wildly.
> - Say at least one encouraging comment per day.
> - If an opportunity comes up, share your faith story.
> - Make a pledge to never let anyone sit alone at lunch.
> - Start a Bible study or prayer group on your campus.
> - Be a person of integrity in everything you say and do.
> - Champion the cause of Christ on your campus!

> - Out of respect for teachers, don't sleep in class or skip.
> - Don't lie, ever!
> - Talk respectfully about your parents.
> - If someone opens up a little, take time to listen.
> - Treat others the way you want to be treated.
> - Initiate conversations with shy people.

Taken from "Dirty Faith, becoming the hands and feet of Jesus." by Audio Adrenaline. Copyright © 2003 by Navpress. Used by permission of Tyndale House Publishers, Inc. All rights reserved.

Memorize: I Peter 5:7 – Cast all your anxiety on Him because He cares about you.

Weekly Challenge: Volunteer at least two weeks at your school. Have a great attitude!

Scripture Reading: Romans 15 – I Corinthians 16

Prayer: Take time daily to pray the revolving prayer calendar – Pray for one thing from your life, your school and your upcoming trip.

Week #10 – Tell

When trying to share your faith with someone, it all starts with a relationship. There are many plans that teach you to share the gospel quickly or with a 1-2-3 approach. I do agree with them biblically, but for the most people (in my opinion) sharing your story with a friend is a more effective means of personal evangelism. This is my simple approach to sharing my faith:

Befriend – Friends listen to friends; they don't often give much merit to a stranger. If you want to share your faith, work on your friendship first.

Build – Work on building bridges. Topics you may have in common you can talk about easily. I believe people can spot someone fake or someone who is trying to sell something, but they are drawn to people who actually care about them.

Bold – Using the bridge you have built on a genuine friendship, discern when the time is right to share your story about what God has done in your life. It takes a bold step of faith to when the Holy Spirit is directing you to start the conversation about things of eternal importance.

One thing to remember: you are not a salesmen trying to sell a product, but rather, it's you sharing your passion about what God has done in your life. You are an example of what God can do in their life, too. Your passion, your authentic faith is what they see in you. Your genuine care for others needs to be REAL!

There are many great websites and apps to help you share your faith. Here are a few:

www.somethingamazing.net

www.shareyourfaithapp.com

www.3story.org

www.iamsecond.com

Memorize: Hebrews 12:2 - Fixing our eyes on Jesus, the pioneer and perfecter of faith. For the joy set before Him, He endured the cross, scorning its shame, and sat down at the right hand of the throne of God.

Weekly Challenge: Practice your story five times out loud. Look for an opportunity to share your story with a family member or a friend.

Scripture Reading: II Corinthians 1 – Galatians 6

Prayer: Take time daily to pray the revolving prayer calendar – Pray for one thing from your life, your school and your upcoming trip.

Week #11 – Fasting and Prayer

1. Before you begin a fast, talk to your parents. If you have a medical condition that require certain foods or caloric intake minimums, seek advice from your doctor before you begin.

2. Fasting is an act of worship, not just giving up food. Fasting and prayer is a time of consecration to God. Consecration is the act of setting oneself apart from the world to be committed to being an instrument of righteousness for God's purposes.

3. Have a clear target as your prayer focus. Write down your vision. (Habakkuk 2:2).

4. Choose a type of fast, prayerfully consider which one to do, then commit to it

* A Daniel fast, with vegetables and water, is good for those with physical demanding jobs.

* A fruit or vegetable fast is a good fast for busy people with demanding jobs. Out of consideration for health issues, supplement with juices and protein drinks.

* A water-only fast. I would not encourage this without strong medical supervision.

5. Prepare yourself a few days before you fast by reducing your intake of food to fruit and vegetables to start the purifying process in your body. Drink lots of water to help your body detoxify. You may experience feelings of impatience, crankiness, and anxiety. You may even experience dizziness and headaches due to lack of food. Your body is working to cleanse itself of impurities. Headaches are very common if you are a coffee or pop drinker.

6. Take the time you normally eat to pray and read the Word.

7. Failing to accomplish the length of fast desired ahead of time does not mean you are a failure; God honors the honest effort, not a certain amount of time.

8. Take a rest everyday if possible, and continue to exercise a little easier than normal.

9. Break the fast slowly over a few days with fruit juice or light soups. Your digestive system slows down, so it can be dangerous if you eat too much too soon.

Memorize: John 10:10 - The thief comes only to steal and kill and destroy; I have come that they may have life, and have it to the full.

Weekly Challenge: Try fasting for a few days, but be safe and talk to your parents first. Ask God for Miracles!

Daily Reading: Ephesians 1 – I Thessalonians 6

Prayer: Take time daily to pray the revolving prayer calendar – Pray for one thing from your life, your school and your upcoming trip.

Week #12 – Live

Blitz Week - Giving God your very best effort!

What is a blitz week: It is a weeklong effort to give God your very best! It's not an experience of Lent, where you give up things, which is also a very powerful journey, but rather a sort of exchange of your time and effort. Instead of giving things up, I want to challenge you to give the time you would spend on other activities to God. You might be surprised how much time that would be.

According to a 2010 Kaiser foundation report, the average American teen spends 7 hours, 38 minutes a day on electronic media devices (TV, internet, computers, phones, etc.), up from 6 hours and 21 minutes in 2004. According to another study (May 2011), the average student spends 60 minutes per day on Facebook, 43 minutes per day searching, and 22 minutes per day on email. Lastly, students reported sending an average of 71 texts per day while doing schoolwork. I am <u>NOT</u> saying these things are bad. I'm saying these habits could get in the way of pursuing God.
(Generation M2: Media in the lives of 8-to18-year olds.)

If you would give God your VERY BEST for one week - what would that look like?

I would like to make a few suggestions:
- Spend time daily in prayer (praying the revolving prayer calendar)
- Spend time in the Word, at this point in the watermark journey, catching up to where you need to be in the New Testament.
- Spend time memorizing the weekly scriptures.
- Spend time reading a quality Christian book that can help you in your pursuit of God.
- Work on your story. Practice it aloud in front of a mirror. Practice in front of others.
- Invest in your relationship with your family: play a game, do a project for your parents, and have fun with a sibling
- Give some time to prayer and fasting
     * Start with a meal, then go to a day, maybe try three days (talk with your parents)
     * Dare I suggest, a media fast: no phone, texting, Facebook, Internet, TV, iPods, movies.
- Meet with others during your fast to pray conversationally

If you gave God your very best, how could your life change?

Memorize: I John 1:9 – If we confess our sins, He is faithful and just and will forgive us our sins and purify us from all unrighteousness.

Weekly Challenge: Write out your Blitz Week plan and give a copy to your coach, pastor, and parents. Now Do it! Be careful! It could change your life!

Daily Reading: II Thessalonians 1 – Titus 3

Prayer: Take time daily to pray the revolving prayer calendar – Pray for one thing from your life, your school and your upcoming trip.

Week #13 - Give

It's been ten weeks since you set your missions goal. It's time to finish it. You may be struggling to think of what to do. Need some inspiration, read Josiah's story.

'When I was in 7th grade, I felt that God wanted me to give $100 to a mission project (Speed the Light). For a 7th grader, that can't get a job, that is a ton of money. I was really nervous at first, but I believed that God was going to help me reach my goal. I started mowing people's yards for money. I wasn't making tons of money but what I did make I started giving in the offering on Wednesdays. I started with just mowing one lawn but when I was faithful in giving that money, God started giving me more lawns to mow. By the end of the summer I had almost reached my goal of $100. As summer ended though I wasn't able to mow lawns anymore, but God gave me other opportunities to make money. At the end of the year I gave over $125. When God first told me to give $100, I didn't think there was anyway I could do that, but in the end, God helped me to give more than He had asked for. In future years I started doing more fundraisers to raise more money. I made homemade pizzas and sold them on a Sunday after church. Each year it became more popular and more and more people wanted to buy them. Every year after that, my personal goal would always be higher than the year before."

Make Giving a Habit

- Give something away periodically, don't lose the ability to let something go that can bless someone in need.
- Budget for giving; pay your 10% tithe, and then give on top of that.
- Be an informed giver; investigate what you are giving to, stay current with their needs as well as their plan of using donations.
- Don't wait to be asked. If you see a need, try and fill it.
- Write out your giving goals and your dream of how you can make a difference. Give a copy of this to your coach and your pastor to talk through it.
- Set a year-long goal. Think of a goal that would stretch you and your youth group.
- Strategize how to accomplish those goals. Talk with your coach about it.

Memorize: Galatians 2:20 - I have been crucified with Christ and I no longer live, but Christ lives in me. The life I now live in the body, I live by faith in the Son of God, who loved me and gave Himself for me.

Weekly Challenge: Finish the goal you set for missions. Prayerfully dream about what your goal can look like for the rest of the year.

Daily Reading: Philemon – James 3

Prayer: Take time daily to pray the revolving prayer calendar – Pray for one thing from your life, your school and your upcoming trip.

Week #14 – Serve

There are many ways you can serve your community. You may need to look for the right opportunity to match your skill set and interest. Everyone can volunteer and make a difference! Here's a list of organizations and ways you could volunteer in your community:

Boys and Girls clubs
Salvation Army
United Way
Red Cross
Hands of Hope - crisis centers
Homeless shelters
Soup kitchen
Organize a coat drive for a local ministry
Food shelf, organize a collection of food shelf items
Nursing homes
Hospital
Churches
Local parks – clean up crews
Highway – clean up crews
Big Brothers, Big Sisters
Schools – as a tutor or mentor
Meals on Wheels
Hospice services
Animal shelter
Special Olympics
Habitat for Humanity
Veteran's home - Volunteer
Gym/field - coach youth sports
Park and Recreation department – volunteer for summer programs

The key - being willing to serve with a great attitude!

Memorize: Romans 5:8 – But God demonstrates His own love in this; while we were still sinners, Christ died for us.

Weekly Challenge: Volunteer at least two hours in your community, with a great attitude.

Scripture Reading: James 4 – I John 5

Prayer: Take time daily to pray the revolving prayer calendar – Pray for one thing from your life, your school and your upcoming trip.

Week #15 – Tell

You have picked a story, you have worked on it with your coach, and you have read it aloud many times. Now, it's time to give it publicly. Ask your youth pastor or leader for a chance to speak in some setting to get experience telling your story. It could be in the youth group or small group, at a Sunday morning service or in a nursing home service. After you have told your story, make some tweaks to it to refine it even more. On most trips, each student has a chance to share publicly what God has done in their life. If at all possible, don't have that be the first time you have ever shared.

Journal
As the trip approaches, start a journal. Record your thoughts and fears leading up to the trip. You can also use it as a Prayer journal: recording how you are praying for the trip. Record how God has answered prayer; list the other students who are going on the trip with you. Consider starting a blog for friends and family to follow on the trip. Visit www.wordpress.com. It is a website that is extremely easy to use, and it will host your blog for free. Just sign up for the free account and start blogging.

Additional questions for developing your story:
- Tell your story from the beginning. How did the Holy Spirit start the desire in your heart to know more about Jesus Christ and what He did for you?
- Describe the details about when you came to admit you were a sinner, believed in your heart that Jesus paid the price for your sins, and made the commit to follow Him as your Lord and Savior?
- How has your life changed after coming to know Christ.
- Explain some of the ups and downs in your walk with Christ.
- Was someone instrumental in your realization of your need for Christ? How did they become involved in the story?
- Describe how God is involved in your everyday life.

Be creative and enjoy the sharing of your personal testimony.

Memorize: Philippians 4:13 - I can do all this through Him who gives me strength.

Weekly Challenge: Look for opportunities to share you faith story publicly. Ask your coach or youth pastor/leader for ideas of how to do this.

Scripture Reading: II John – Revelations 22

Prayer: Take time daily to pray the revolving prayer calendar – Pray for one thing from your life, your school and your upcoming trip.

(Congratulations! You just read the entire New Testament in 15 weeks)

A Post-Trip Challenge

The trip is now over. How was it? Was it incredible? Did you eat balut or somewhat raw bacon with the hair still on it? Did you take a subway at rush hour or zip line through the rainforest? Did you walk on a glacier or climb the stairs of a pyramid? Whatever your cultural experiences were, they have left stains on your life. You may never return to your trip destination, but for the rest of your life, you will be able to describe your experiences in great detail. The sights, smells, and sounds, as well as the emotions you had welling up within you, will spill out when the ministry, country, or city is mentioned in conversation. You will find yourself smiling, talking a little faster and louder when you can talk as a first-hand witness about the location. I know because this happens to me all the time. If you want to see me light up, start talking about places that I've been. Engaging others in a spirited conversation about memories I have is truly a passion of mine.

You are now an expert on the location of your trip because you have walked the streets, saw the sights, interacted with the locals, and become emotionally attached to the places; the memories will forever be etched in your mind. Add the spiritual aspects of the trip and you have a chance for life-long change! For many people, the trip is the high spiritual mark of their life. They have stepped out in faith and conquered their fear of ministering, and God blessed them for it. It has left a watermark on their life. The big question now: Now What?

The memories of your trip will fade over time, but the pursuit of Christ does not need to fade. In fact, instead of it being a one-time, spiritual high, it can become the norm for your life. A dependence on God, boldness in your faith, and a willingness to serve others can now become routine in your daily life. Remember these principles found in chapter two.

Live It – To continue the pursuit of Christ in your daily time in the Bible and connect with Him in prayer to continue to build that personal relationship.

Live It Out Loud – To continue to share your story with those around you while constantly looking for opportunities to serve those around you. Always be open to giving yourself to others without expecting anything in return.

The foreign or domestic mission trip is now over; the pursuit of Christ, steps of faith in ministry, and dependency on Him does not need to be. If you can view your present location as your mission field, God will continue to use you as His voice for those who need His divine help. The problems you were first-hand witnesses to on your trip are at home, too. Drug and alcohol abuse, violence, and hopelessness are all around you, but it's so easy to turn a blind eye when problems exist in our hometown. If you can do something bold for God on a mission trip, I'm confident you can do something bold for God at home, too.

Adopt your campus as your current mission field. Everyday, you walk past students and teachers that struggle with the same problems you were so concerned about on your trip. God is calling you to take a stand for Him on your campus! He doesn't need to send a believer from a foreign country to come and learn the language and become knowledgeable about the local culture and habits of students. He has already sent you! You are the expert to the local culture and the key to reaching your campus, not someone else. God has placed you there for such a time as this.

Esther was the queen in a godless society under King Xerxes. A plot was uncovered to conduct genocide of the Jewish people in the kingdom. Queen Esther was a Jew, but she kept this secret from the king. Her uncle, Mordecai approached Esther and reminded her of the reason she had risen to power in the kingdom. Esther 4:12-14 says, "When Esther's words were reported to Mordecai, he sent back this answer: "Do not think that because you are in the king's house you alone of all the Jews will escape. For if you remain silent at this time, relief and deliverance for the Jews will arise from another place, but you and your father's family will perish. And who knows but that you have come to your royal position for such a time as this?"

I believe that God has placed you on your campus for "such a time as this!" You have experienced a mission trip of God's favor; it's now time to apply that same effort and dedication you had leading up to the trip; step out in faith and see God do amazing things on your campus!

Agreeing with Mordecai's words to Esther, **I believe You have been placed on your campus, for such a time as this**!

God is ready to use you to reach your present mission field. Are you ready?

Daily Journal, Day #1

Daily Journal, Day #2

Daily Journal, Day #4

Daily Journal, Day #5

Daily Journal, Day #6

Daily Journal, Day #7

Daily Journal, Day #9

Daily Journal, Day #11

Daily Journal, Day #12

Daily Journal, Day #13

Daily Journal, Day #14

Author Biographies

Sarah is a Registered Nurse working at the St Cloud Hospital in their float pool. She loves going on mission trips and working with youth. In her spare time, she enjoys doing crafts, watching movies, and spending time with her family!

Kathy lives in a rural community in Minnesota on a small hobby farm with her husband and two small children (Adah, age 5 and Caleb age 2). She works as a physician assistant at a local clinic. Her hobbies include: spending time with her family, gardening, spending time outdoors, and taking care of her sheep, goats, chickens, cats, and dog.

Mark recently married to his high school sweetheart, Ruthann. He enjoys making people laugh and having a fun time with friends and family.

Sarah is married and has two beautiful children, a boy and a girl. She claims to have the best job in the world; she gets to stay at home with her children everyday and wouldn't trade that for anything! She loves spending time with her family and friends and playing and laughing with her children; they're hilarious!

Lukas is a first year student at North Central University. He loves playing sports, with hockey being his favorite. He is the oldest of four boys, and his all-time favorite drink is sweet tea. In his free time, he loves hanging out with his friends and family.

Steve is a middle school principal in Minnesota. When he is not at school, he loves to spend time with his wife and two daughters. He is an avid Minnesota sports fan and rarely misses a Golden Gopher basketball game.

Sarah spends her time enjoying life in a small town dubbed the Apple Capital of Minnesota with her husband, Masanoni. When they aren't at home, they are likely exploring the rest of God's incredible creations around the world!

Kelly is blessed to have two amazing little girls that have shown God's love in a way she has never comprehended before! She has a supportive and caring husband who has taught her to always look at things wisely. She is privileged to work as a social worker helping children and their families who have experienced severe trauma in their lives. Spending time in nature, appreciating all God has given us, is one of her favorite things to do!

Matt is a happily married man who works as a service advisor for a car dealership. He enjoys spending time with his wife, fishing, watching movies, and hanging out with friends.

Travis grew up in rural Minnesota and upon graduation, enlisted in the army. He is currently serving in U.S. Special Forces and lives in Tennessee.

Holly grew up in a Christian family in central Minnesota and has always wanted to use her gifts to honor God. During her senior year in college, she felt called to study and teach the New Testament; her deepest desire is to see the people of God understand the Bible and integrate it well in their own lives and communities. Holly married her best friend, Max, after seminary, and the last nine years have been a flurry of PhD work, teaching college and seminary classes, and parenting two little boys, Noah and Moses.

Jess developed her a passion for missions and giving early on in life, through God. Her passion for missions has directed many of her major life decisions. She traveled on two trips during high school and later spent a year in Norway before pursuing a career in pharmacy where she continues to invest in medical missions around the world.

Rachel is married to her awesome husband Kevin, and together they are expecting their first child. She works as a registered nurse in surgery at the University of Minnesota Hospital. Some of her favorite activities to do are, biking, running, going on long walks with her husband, being outside, crafting, traveling, and hanging out with her sisters.

Will is married to Alleks and live in Central Minnesota where he works as a Youth Pastor.

Kelsey has a love for volleyball, her favorite sport. She also enjoys going on vacations and traveling the world. Photography is a hobby she enjoys, especially when she is traveling and experiencing new places.

Julie has worked three years as a Starbucks barista and as a result, has turned into a coffee addict, so naturally, she can usually be found with a cup o' joe in her hand, reading a good book (if her two sons, Gabriel and Malachi, allow it). Her husband, Jeff, is the pastor of an Evangelical Free Church, and on the rare occasion that they get a night out, they like to go to a nice restaurant where they usually end up talking about how cute their kids are.

Allen is married to his college sweetheart Becky for 20 years; together they have two wonderful children, Jack and Leah. He is an Anesthesiologist, is active in his church, currently teaching 5-8 grades, and was a Major in the Air Force. He enjoys coaching his kids. Participating in medical missions/sports missions trip in the near future is one of his goals.

Riley is currently a sophomore in high school. He enjoys competing for his school in soccer, basketball, and track. He is nearly unstoppable at NCAA football 14 on PS3 and fills his spare time by hanging out with his family and friends.

Allysa has had a heart for missions. After high school, she worked for a missions organization based out of Florida for 4 years, and with them, travelled to 15 different countries. She currently works as a Property manager for income based housing in her hometown, her new mission field. She enjoys cooking, gardening, art projects and playing with her beautiful little girl, that just turned two years old.

Sam has been married to his best friend Juliene for over ten years and is the father of four great kids. He has over 15 years experience in youth ministry as a volunteer leader and youth pastor. He loves helping students hear God's voice and step out in obedience.

Jacinta spends a lot of her time is spent teaching science to junior high students. When she is not at school, she and her husband like to spend time with their many family members and friends. They feel so blessed to be a part of a small group where they can continue to grow in their relationships with the Lord as they support and encourage each other through life's seasons.

Jake is a senior in high school. He plans on attending North Central University where he plans on pursuing a teaching degree. He loves soccer and will play next year at the University. He enjoys disc golfing, basketball, and dominating in FIFA 14.

Shannon is venturing into new territory by starting her own business as a Nutritional Therapist, while working with her parents at their salon and spa. She loves soaking up every moment with close friends and family enjoying good food, going on a good run to test her limits, and stirring the creative juices.

Rachel is currently working as a loan officer at Wells Fargo Home Mortgage, and is married to her husband, Andrew. Her favorites include: playing tennis with her husband, running, and drinking coffee. Rachel and Andrew hope to do long-term missions work in Mexico someday soon.

Josiah lives in Bemidji with his wife Emily. He is a Youth Pastor at Crossroads Church. He loves to play soccer, disc golf, hunt, and fish, but he especially loves it when he can use those things to lead people to Jesus.

Phil is a Missionary with the Assemblies of God World Missions. He lives in Stockholm, Sweden, along with his wife, Katja, and their three wonderful children. The main focus in the country is to encourage church planting and pioneering University groups.

Christina is a wife, mother, Jesus follower, and coffee lover. Christina has been married for over eight years to Jason, and together they have four beautiful children. She enjoys camping, running, watching baseball, drinking coffee, conversing, and spending time with her family.

Jen has her dream life. She is married to her best friend Bobby and together they have three boys and a daughter. She spends her days teaching a classroom full of energetic second graders. In her spare time, she loves to watch her kids compete in sports and go on dates with her husband of 21 years.

Kesiah and he husband live in Minnesota with their 3 children. She works with women who have developmental disabilities. Kesiah and husband Danny have their own business in the southern suburbs of the Twin Cities.

Credits

Rideout, Victoria J, Ulla G. Foehr, and Donald F. Roberts. "Generation M2: Media in the Lives of 8 to 18 Year Olds." (*The Henry J. Kaiser Family Foundation*) (January 2010). Abstract. *Eric.* Web. 6 Jan. 2014.

Thanks for taking the time to read and work through this project. My prayer is that your mission trip will be truly life-changing, and that you will have a permanent stain on your life. A watermark that will be evident for the rest of your life!

If you would like to talk or have questions about anything in the book concerning missions Contact me on facebook or: minnesotayouthalive@yahoo.com

Sincerely,
Bobby Loukinen

Made in the USA
San Bernardino, CA
06 February 2014